Praise for Tony Weedor and *The Reason for Tears*

"Tony Weedor's smile and out-going personality belie the pain and loss he has experienced in his life. His story is gripping and challenging—I couldn't put it down. He is honest and vulnerable but his intellect is keen as he tackles—with grace and humor—some of the most important issues facing the Christian church today. His Christian faith has been tested in ways I can only shudder to think about. He has much to teach us about being an intelligent, faithful believer in Christ."

—RUTH GRAHAM

"What a page-turner! Tony Weedor's suspense-filled story, from his life as a Muslim country boy in a peaceful…West Africa, to the heartache of being disowned by his family for a Christian conversion and marriage, to the family's desperate plights and terrors during the atrocities of the Liberian Civil War, followed by prolonged refugee life, all the way through to an American seminary education, and finally to a return home… *The Reason for Tears* will have you in tears of joy by the end. A more astonishing tribute to the greatness and grace of God could scarcely be found."

—CRAIG L. BLOMBERG, DISTINGUISHED PROFESSOR OF NEW TESTAMENT, DENVER SEMINARY

"Tony Weedor is an African Ravi Zacharias."

—Terry Futrell, Author, Consultant, and Former Program Manager Y-12 National Security Complex, Oak Ridge

THE REASON
FOR TEARS

THE REASON FOR TEARS

TONY WEEDOR
with Andy Straka

Carpenter's Son Publishing

The Reason for Tears: A Memoir

© 2019 by Tony Weedor

Published by Carpenter's Son Publishing, Franklin, Tennessee

Published in association with Larry Carpenter of Christian Book Services, LLC
www.christianbookservices.com

Scripture taken from THE HOLY BIBLE, NEW INTERNATIONAL VERSION®, NIV® Copyright © 1973, 1978, 1984, 2011 by Biblica, Inc.™ Used by permission. All rights reserved worldwide.

Cover and Interior Design by Suzanne Lawing

Cover photo courtesy of Rebekah Musser, Bekah Imagery

Edited by David Brown

Printed in the United States of America

978-1-949572-62-9

"The truth is that there are such things as Christian tears, and too few of us ever weep them."

John Stott

Contents

INTRODUCTION

I wasn't living in America on September 11, 2001. I remember glancing out the classroom window at the late afternoon sun baking the hills surrounding Addis Ababa, capital of Ethiopia, where I was teaching Islamic history at Evangelical Theological College. September 11 was Enkutatash, the "gift of jewels," the first day of the year on the Ethiopian calendar. In preparation for celebrations that evening, the floral aroma of Ethiopian coffee—prepared in the traditional way in a clay pot known as a jebena—drifted like a balm on the air. I was working then for SIM International, originally known as Sudan Interior Mission, a global interdenominational Christian missionary organization. As a former Muslim, I also lectured on Islam at another university.

In the middle of my lesson, a commotion arose in the hallway. All eyes turned toward the sound as a young student's wide-eyed face appeared in the doorway. He was waving his hands in the air. "Come! Come listen to the radio! America is under attack!"

My class immediately ended for the day. Chairs scraped as I followed my students out into the hallway to find out what was going on. Looking at my watch, I realized it was still early morning seven thousand miles away in the United States. To me, America was not some far-off foreign land. As a refugee and immigrant from Liberia in West Africa, I had lived in

Colorado for more than eight years, where I'd worked and earned my master of divinity (MDiv) from Denver Seminary before coming to serve as a missionary in Ethiopia.

My wife and I were grateful to America, the nation and culture that had generously adopted us and allowed us to escape the horror of war in our native country. Three of my four children had been born in the United States. With no small concern then, I made my way down the corridor to a common area where a crowd had already gathered around a large radio.

For what seemed like hours, we listened in transfixed horror as the live BBC coverage of the terrorist airliner attacks unfolded. We could only imagine the image of the first of the two World Trade Center towers in New York City collapsing into a mushrooming plume of rubble and smoke, followed not much later by the second tower. According to the British announcer, thousands of people were still trapped inside those buildings. I couldn't believe what I was hearing—the chaos and random senselessness of it all.

Death is a robe everyone has to wear, an old African proverb goes. To my students, I was not like other missionaries teaching at the school. Like them, I was from Africa. They even referred to me as Tamrat, which in Amharic, Ethiopia's main language, means "miracle," because I was one of few emigrants who'd returned to Africa. Not only had I grown up in Africa, I knew what it was like to walk in fear of my life, to be starving, and to witness unspeakable, inhuman things.

I exchanged glances with a few other faculty members, who pursed their mouths and shook their heads sadly. I suppose many of us sensed what was happening, but the gravity and full impact of the situation had yet to set in. Already there was some speculation on the radio about Islamic terrorism.

My world seemed to shift in time and space as I tried to comprehend all that was taking place.

Even more shocking, the reaction of some of my students stunned me. A number of them were smiling. A few even cheered at the devastation and death we were hearing about from an ocean away. What were they thinking?

From the events of that day forward, we entered unchartered territory when it came to America and Africa and uncharted global territory when it came to Christianity and Islam. My students at the Evangelical Theological College were non-Muslim. To them, America was simply an unassailable worldwide power, at times benevolent, but mostly disinterested in their lives, a nation for which they felt a begrudging respect tempered by suspicion.

At first, I was flummoxed by the way they'd reacted to the attacks on New York City and Washington, DC. In conversations with them over the next several days and weeks, however, I discovered rivers of resentment that were deeper than I realized. Many of my students looked upon the United States, like Western Europe, as a distant and often arrogant colonial power. What's more, I'd seen something else in their eyes as they gathered around the radio on 9/11. Having grown up Muslim in rural West Africa, it felt all too familiar.

Fear.

Fear lay at the heart of their response to the attacks of that day. If America could be brutally assaulted in such a way, how could anyone anywhere be safe?

Over the next few days and months, I did my best to represent the truth to my students, not just trying to present a clearer and more balanced picture of America, but the kindness I personally had experienced from Americans and the

American church. We talked about the experiences I'd had living with my family in Colorado.

More importantly, we talked about the difference between religion and relationship and the importance of a personal relationship with a God who is not some distant deity, but came to earth and lived among human beings in the person of Jesus Christ, who offers salvation and freedom from fear to all who will call on his name. For some, this is a hard grace to accept. We want so badly to recreate God in our own image and try reaching God on our own.

Fear does unexpected things to people. It often causes them to behave in unpredictable ways. I've seen this happen in Africa and in the world of Islam. It may be difficult for those who haven't grown up in such cultures to fully understand just how powerful an influence fear can have on people's lives and worldviews.

Over the next several months, the regular news broadcasts we received via radio and occasional TV were dominated by reporting about the American Bush administration's aptly-named "War on Terror" and the anti-terror efforts of its British and Western allies. I grew frustrated sometimes by interviews and commentary from so-called "experts" on religion who attempted to equate Christianity and Islam. Some even went so far as to talk about a repeat of the medieval Crusades. At the end of 2001, an American-led coalition invaded Afghanistan in search of the stronghold of Osama bin Laden, the mastermind behind the 9/11 attacks. Less than eighteen months later, America also invaded Iraq, then under Saddam Hussein's regime.

Returning with my family to Colorado at the end of 2003, I realized right away we'd come back to a changed America.

Mostly gone by then were the thousands upon thousands of American flags that had flown around the country in the wake of the 9/11 attacks. But much of the confusion, fear, and suspicion remained. It seemed like everybody—pastors, churches, even those at my seminary—wanted to talk with me about Islam, to try to understand what could motivate such hatred and terror.

As in Ethiopia, I did my best to explain. But I had more work to do to better understand the spiritual and emotional implications of 9/11 and the war on terror. For that fuller understanding, I would not find a catalyst in America. I would need to return to Liberia, land of my birth. It was a land that was itself still reeling from the horror of two devastating civil wars.

I would go there in hope of resurrecting one of the most important relationships in my life. I would also relive my own deliverance from some of the deep-seated fears with which I'd grown up.

Tony Weedor
Charlottesville, Virginia
June, 2019

PROLOGUE

I think I may know why God created tears. I think I may know because I came into this world in a country full of rain, a newborn crying on a blanket in the monsoon mud behind our hut on a Liberian army base where my soldier father was stationed. One day I would come to see those seasonal downpours as heaven's tears for everything God knew was about to come.

Now more than forty years later, sitting in the back of a Toyota Land Cruiser in a slum outside the Liberian capital of Monrovia, I couldn't help but ask myself why I'd come back to Liberia at all. *What if Mama still refuses to speak to me? What will we even say to one another after more than fifteen years?*

The Bible says God weeps for our pain. Had God shared my tears when Mama and my Muslim father cast me out for becoming a Christian? Or later when I watched so many of my fellow Liberians die through civil wars or witnessed the 9/11 attacks from afar? No one had ever told me I would nearly curse God and whimper with people in their deaths. No one had told me tears could be for comfort or that their silent sounds could be my best confession or why tears would be my one and only plea with God to look again, to care.

I wanted to believe such terrible things were in the past, but now that I was here again, I recognized they would be forever part of me, as though my life has been one complete knowing of things to come, of things already gone. How could I say I understood when no one really can?

The car slowed as we neared our destination. Dozens of children, who seemed to have been watching for us, poured from adjacent streets and alleyways to surround our vehicle. There were so many, our driver was forced to stop. They were singing, jumping, laughing, and dancing with hands raised. I could hardly believe it. Many had bloated bellies from malnutrition, but that didn't seem to keep them from greeting us in celebration.

Younger children ran around in circles as if they didn't know what to do with their bodies, their matchstick arms clothed in colorful T-shirts that hung from their shoulders like so many decorative flags. Their coal-black skin matched my own, and as I waved through the window glass, I saw in them a reflection of my younger self.

Before I had more time to pray through my fears, my sister Victoria appeared among the children. I rolled the window down.

"You made it!" She had to yell to be heard over the bedlam of young voices.

I smiled. "I guess we found the correct neighborhood."

"Of course! You're in the right place."

"Wonderful." I tried not to sound as apprehensive as I felt. I couldn't shake the feeling that maybe this was all some sort of setup, some kind of dream.

She looked around at all the children singing and dancing. "As you can see, word travels fast around here."

"Is everything all right?"

"Yes, Tony. I think we're ready. Mama says she will see you now."

CHAPTER ONE

The Weight of Love

Months earlier, I awoke to cold air streaming down on me as our flight from North Carolina began its final descent into Denver, Colorado. It was January 2004. My wife Beth and I with our children had recently returned from four years of ministry in Ethiopia. We had spent the last week at SIM International headquarters in Charlotte, N.C., where we all received medical checkups and Beth and I were debriefed about our time in Africa.

I had also accepted an offer from SIM leader Dr. Steve Strauss to serve as SIM International research director for Islam, which would involve teaching missionaries who were preparing to serve in Africa or in other regions among Muslim populations. Better yet, the job would allow us to live back here in Denver where I'd gone to seminary and where we'd been living prior to going to Ethiopia.

I reached up to turn off the overhead air. Next to me, Beth's shoulders rose and fell with the rhythm of her breathing, a strand of hair falling across her forehead. Her face was as beautiful in sleep as the day we'd first met.

Yawning, I looked out the window. The snow-covered Front Range of the Rockies punched holes through low clouds in the distance, rising above a terracotta plain. Across the aisle, exhausted but excited to be back where they'd spent their early childhood, our children slept next to one another in their seats. Abigail, the oldest and about to begin high school, was outgoing and determined. Alieya was the quiet, steady one, our reader. Then came witty Antoinette, who was never afraid to speak her mind. The youngest, our only son, Tony, was a natural leader, patient and caring.

As the plane banked to begin its approach, glistening-white peaks backdropped the Denver skyline, and I could just about pick out the neighborhood on the outskirts of the city where we would be living. I should have been as excited about our return as the children. I had so many good memories of the welcoming, generous people we'd met in Denver, including my colleagues at the seminary, who'd supported us and been so patient with me after our arrival in America fourteen years before.

But as much as I wanted to take in the excitement of our return and experience the joys of my new calling, my thoughts kept rushing back to Africa, not to Ethiopia, but to the rolling hills and rainforests of my native country from the Wologisi and Nimba mountains to the coastal plain with its swamps and tidal marshes to Liberia's beautiful seashore beaches. The reason was clear to me now. I couldn't stop thinking about my mother.

I hadn't seen Mama, my only surviving parent, since 1989. I'd prayed over Genesis 32 and 33—the story of Jacob's reconciliation with Esau—many times, and I couldn't help wondering if I, like Jacob in Genesis, had unfinished business with someone I loved.

"Some of your family is still out to get you," Beth had reminded me. "You don't know what you'd be going into if you went back there. Someone might even try to kill you."

What if she was right? After all, Liberia could feel at times like the most impossible of countries, a nation founded by former American slaves, known as Americo-Liberians, who'd used their superior education and trade connections to gain political control a century and a half before—only to repeat the sins of their former American slave masters by oppressing the native country people like me.

Muslim families like mine were in the minority, Liberia being a country where the Christian religion, extravagant in its flamboyance, held sway, at least on the surface. Complicating matters further, religion in Liberia—both Muslim and Christian—was mixed with local traditions, superstitions, and the teachings of secret bush societies, animism, and voodoo. Ritualistic initiations, revenge killings, and forced genital mutilations still occurred with regularity, and at Christmastime, bush devils still danced in the streets.

If all of that weren't enough, sixteen different native tribes vied for position and dominance in Liberia. My father's Belle tribe was one of the smallest. My mother's Mandingo tribe, on the other hand, was a sizeable ethnic group all across West Africa. In Liberia, Mandingoes made up nearly 7 percent of the population. But though many centuries had passed since their migration into Liberia—certainly long before the Americo-Liberians—they were still considered foreigners by many other Liberians because they practiced Islam instead of Christianity.

Before we'd left Ethiopia to return to America, Beth had

asked me what I was going to do about my desire to see Mama again. I'd told her I didn't know, but now I realized that in my heart, where it counted, I *did* know.

In my earliest memories, I am riding on Mama's back. Soft and strong at the same time, in the way of a proud Mandingo woman, she carted me everywhere. As her stride rocked me gently, I would bury my cheek in her headscarf.

A merchant, Mama grew and harvested kola nuts. She planted tobacco, corn, onions, and peppers, too, selling them in the marketplace, along with palm oil and other items. With the ups and downs of my ex-military father's rice farm, Mama was our family's only consistent source of income. She taught my brothers and sisters and me how to garden. She taught us how to raise chickens. She worked as if she bore the weight of love for our entire family, striving against the heat and oppression of a Liberia that at the time treated its native citizens as if we were inferior second-class citizens.

As the plane descended into Denver, I wondered how much more striving Mama could bear. I knew she was still alive, but I could only imagine the toll the past fifteen years of strife and Liberian civil war had taken on her.

I thought I felt her calling me home.

CHAPTER TWO

Fire and Rice

Though I was born in 1960 on a Liberian army base, I grew up in Belle Balumah (Balumah for short), a village in the plateau highlands of Liberia, where my father had turned to farming after his service in the Liberian Army. We spoke English and the Belle language at home. My siblings and I referred to our parents as "Mi nu Te" in Belle or simply Mama and Papa in English.

I was the middle child of five born to Forkpah and Manifah Gbejoe Weedor. They christened me Anthony Abdullah Kono Weedor. When I was young, I was often referred to as Kono, which means "chosen" or Number One. My first and last English names were to be used for school and in Liberian society. My Muslim name was for praying and the mosque. My four other siblings were my older sister MJ, my older brother Austin, my younger brother Alfred, who was next in age after me, and my sister Victoria, the youngest.

We Muslims were a minority in predominately Christian Liberia, making up less than 15 percent of the country's population. Once I began to walk, Mama took to playfully calling me "Distance," because, she told everyone who would listen, no matter how hard she tried to hold on to me, I would always turn and run away.

Our culture was misogynistic, meaning men were typically elevated above women and women were often treated poorly. As I grew up and began attending school, I came to understand that this was wrong. My privilege of being male wouldn't shield me, however, from family rejection, which I would one day come to know all too well.

Where we lived in rural Liberia, there were no roads or automobiles, only mile after mile of hills, grassland, and rainforest. It took two to three days to travel to the capital city, Monrovia, mostly walking on forest trails. Our village of Balumah was home to a few hundred people. Since we were the Liberian district headquarters, we had a small jungle airstrip, but it was rarely used. Plane trips cost too much money.

Our transistor radios connected us to the outside world— Monrovia, the BBC, and the Voice of America—and the batteries to keep them running were a precious commodity. Replacing them might take days or weeks, so we would always remove the batteries after listening to the radio to help lengthen their life. Sometimes people would even put them in the sun in the mistaken belief the sunlight helped recharge them.

I've already mentioned how much my mother taught me. My father taught us other things. With him, we farmed and hunted wild game. We learned how to handle tools and weapons. We learned about fear and respect for the jungle and poisonous cobras lurking in the trees. We learned respect for authority—above all, his!

I also learned from my parents that to deal with my fears required me to pray to Allah five times per day, reciting prayers in Arabic, a language I didn't speak and only selectively understood. In addition, I would be admitted as a boy into Poro, a secret Liberian hunting and traditional religious society presided over by witch doctors. I would learn to rely on its mystical elements, amulets, and rituals for protection, healing, and even to potentially make me invincible when facing the dangers of the wild.

Over centuries, the animism and pagan rituals of our native culture had intermixed with Muslim teachings to form a hybrid folk Islam. It was a way of life built around ritual, rote practices, and physical elements believed to have supernatural powers in order to keep demons, disease, and bad luck from hurting or overpowering us. Like almost every other African Muslim then, I was taught growing up to be afraid of many things.

***

I was about four years old when I did something the rest of my family would never let me forget.

I remember squatting that morning over a circle of rocks in our "rice kitchen," a storage shed used to house our family's freshly harvested rice on our farm, which was an hour-long walk from our village. I peered at the smoldering remains of the morning's cooking fire, the heat and smoke from which also helped dry the rice all around me.

There wasn't much left of the fire, just a couple charred pieces of wood mixed with burnt ash, out of which a whiff of smoke rose to disappear toward the ceiling. I had nothing else to occupy my attention at the moment, and I was missing my wood-carved toys, the mud walls and thatched straw roof of our home in the village, the smell of goats and cattle and cooking fires cooling in the late morning, and Mama's colorful dried vegetables banging in the breeze against the drying rail.

Through the open door of the rice kitchen, I could see the fields surrounded by wind-tossed trees where Mama and Papa were working with dozens of others to bring in the harvest. The rhythmic sound of machetes chopping at the rice stalks was punctuated by the chirp-chirp-chirping of pepper birds. A gust of wind swirled into the shed, stirring a piece of burlap that hung from an opening in the roof.

Curious about the fire, I poked a piece of bamboo deeper into the ash to see what might happen. Nothing did, so I nudged the stick deeper into the coals. Outside, a parrot squawked from the direction of the river. One of the many tributaries of the St. Paul River basin flowing down from the Guinea highlands into our country, it coursed for mile after mile through hills and rainforest before descending to the coastal plain.

There it met up with the main river, eventually flowing through mangrove and swamp to Monrovia before finally emptying into the Atlantic. I'd never seen the ocean, but my parents had described how its vast waters stretched beyond the horizon and waves crashed onto the beaches day and night, the power of its fierce undertow pulling against the monkey fruit and baobab of the jungle, the rhythms of the sub-Saharan monsoon already building toward the end of this dry season in the clouds.

I moved the stick again. Mama had told me she was glad the rice harvest would soon be over. Out in the fields, I could hear women singing and men calling out to one another, laughing. After cutting the stalks, the harvesters gathered them into great bundles and tossed them on to large wooden platforms. Mama and my older sisters had shown me the cuts and bruises on their feet from standing barefoot on the platforms, rolling the stalks over and over against the wood to thresh the rice.

To ready the crop for storage, my father and other men from neighboring farms would build huge outdoor fires alongside the platforms. The outdoor fires were used for preliminary drying of the thousands of kernels before packing them into cloth bags and stacking them in the rice kitchens.

The kitchens stood together in one long row, one structure per family. Rice was the staple of our diet. By the time the harvest ended, each structure would hold more than enough grain to supply a family for the year. The walls of my family's kitchen had almost disappeared behind the stacked-up bags of rice.

So far, I wasn't having much success with my bamboo stick. But I'd also brought a pile of straw inside in case I couldn't get it to light. Sweating in the heat and humidity, I pulled the bamboo out and looked at it several times, but nothing seemed to be happening. Maybe I was doing something wrong. I could hear the wind growing stronger outside, but I ignored it. I poked my stick in again, this time even deeper among the coals.

Seconds later to my delight, a larger puff of smoke arose from among the embers. The bamboo caught fire. It looked just like the fire from the big blaze the adults had built outside. I pulled my stick out and stared into the flame. I waved the bamboo back and forth, loving how the fire danced in my hand.

But now, the flame was creeping down the stick closer to my hand. Without thinking, I tossed its charred remains behind me. Emboldened by my success, I turned toward the embers again to try again with another stick. I was so engrossed in my coals and the second bamboo stick that I failed to notice the stick I'd tossed to the floor had set fire to the pile of straw I'd brought inside. I didn't notice either when the licking flames reached the stacked bags of rice.

Once they ignited, however, the dry rice made for a perfect fuel. Before I realized what was happening, I heard someone shout from outside. I looked up to see a large amount of smoke billowing toward the ceiling. Spinning around, I discovered that the entire wall of rice behind me was on fire.

I was terrified. I had no idea what to do. With no shoes on my feet to try to stamp out the flames, I panicked, dropping the second bamboo stick and raced outside to escape the smoke.

More shouts of alarm rang out. Now I could see people running toward me from all directions. I started to cry. Smoke was already beginning to fill the air above the line of rice kitchens, rising into the late morning sky. I turned back to look at our rice kitchen and stared through tears at the growing fire.

A man ran up carrying a big bucket of water. He tossed the water at the fire, but his effort barely made a dent in the rising inferno. Several more adults arrived. Some began to panic, no doubt worried about the fate of their own rice kitchens. Barely pausing to throw me angry glares, they started throwing water on the adjacent rice kitchens to keep them from going up in flames too. Men, women, and children were all running back and forth to the river with buckets, doing their best to keep the flames confined. But the fire continued to consume what was left of our rice kitchen. There was nothing more they could do. I dropped to my knees, wracked with sobs. Mama and Papa were going to kill me. One older woman I knew grabbed me by the arm and began to shake me, but I jumped to my feet and wriggled free of her grip. Many in the crowd, their faces covered in ash and sweat, were yelling and pointing fingers at me now. Out of the corner of my eye, I caught sight of Mama running toward us from the fields with my baby brother on her back. If looks could kill, I'd have already been dead. Someone else reached out to try to grab me, but I escaped again. I turned my back on all of them and fled.

I sprinted as far and as fast as my young legs would carry me. My eyes filled with tears and I could barely see in front of me, let alone where I was going. Crashing through the undergrowth, I dodged among tall trees, scraping my arms and legs on the rough trunks. At some point, I became aware of Mama running close behind me. She must have left my baby brother to be watched by someone. She was big, she was fast, and she was gaining on me. I felt her white-hot rage.

Bursting into an open field, I cried out in fear. Seconds later, Mama plowed into me, the force of her running legs knocking both of us to the ground.

My lungs gave out. I could run no more. Drenched in sweat and bleeding, I rolled over and lay on my back in the grass, my chest heaving. Mama lay next to me. At some point, without me even being aware, her whipcord arms, made strong from years of hard labor, locked onto my waist. She was crying and screaming my name into my ear. She started to swat me on the back of the head.

But no sooner had her blows begun to land than they stopped. A moment later, I felt another pair of hands on me.

My grandmother Zinnah stood over us like a boxing referee separating a pair of locked fighters. Resigned to Grandma's intervention, Mama let go of me as soon as Zinnah pushed us apart.

Old but still powerful, Grandmother pulled me to my feet, moved in front of me, and stared defiantly at Mama. "If anyone lays a hand on this boy, they lay a hand on me!"

Mama glared at her. To this day, I can still see her trembling with rage, since she dared not challenge my grandmother. I could only imagine how frustrated she must have felt. Mama let out a guttural wail that echoed across the field and back through the jungle.

Trying somehow to process my good fortune, I stood frozen to the spot. Mucus poured from my nose and mouth. My legs were bloody, and my face was covered in dirt and tears. Part of me wanted to run away again, but I realized that wasn't going to happen. Grandmother's fingers were still locked onto my shoulders, and her hands weighed down on me like heavy bags of rice. Without another word, she spun me around and began marching me back toward the angry crowd.

Back by the fields, the fire had been brought under control, but all that was left of our family's rice kitchen was a smoking ruin. The acrid smell of burnt rice filled the air. People milled around, shouting. They were looking for someone to blame, and I was exactly the person they were looking for. Lucky for me, my father, who had just received word of the fire, was still too far away on an adjoining farm to get his hands on me. But that didn't stop the rest of the villagers from voicing their rage and demands for punishment.

Grandma led me in front of the crowd. Everyone grew silent, staring at me as if I'd committed a murder, which given the importance of the crop we all needed to survive, I might as well may have. And it wouldn't just be our family who suffered. The entire village would. In our tribal tradition, everyone would have to come together and share from his or her own supplies of rice to help feed my family and make up for the loss.

Some of the older men reached for large sticks, the kind I'd seen them use before to beat children. In my father's absence, I was afraid I might receive worse than a beating. But Grandma Zinnah kept me close by her side. Fear of her wrath may have been the only thing keeping me alive.

She repeated to the crowd the same stern warning she'd given to Mama, and it had much the same impact. No one wanted to mess with a tribal elder like Zinnah. But then she went one step further. I was covered head to toe in sweat, soot, and mud, not to mention the blood on my legs and feet from crashing through the bush. Zinnah picked up one of the large buckets of water people had been using to fight the fire. She told me to stand still.

There in front of the whole village, she began to pour cool water over my head, bathing me in much the same way as my mother had done many times before. The river water was cold. I shivered and sobbed. Mama, standing next to us, sobbed too.

The message to the village was clear. Grandma Zinnah saw me as something more precious than the rice harvest.

The cold water became my salvation as I stood in the glare of the crowd's anger and pointing fingers, crying and spluttering with shame. Years later, I would recall every detail, how Grandma Zinnah's love gave me a glimmer of a much greater love, a love that would come from one of the last places I'd ever expect. The men threw down their sticks and returned to the fields. The angry women began to turn away. Gradually, the crowd dispersed while Zinnah whispered softly in my ear, "Kono, you must never forget this day. Remember how special you are and never, ever play with fire again."

***

From then on, fear became my constant companion. Some time later, when I was five or six, I remember standing in a jungle thicket with my father, a heavy spear in my hand though I was barely strong enough to hold up its weight. The grass was so deep I could barely move. We had startled a giant forest hog from its hiding place, and I watched, terrified, as only a few yards away it turned its tusked face toward us, chuffing and pawing the ground.

Next to me, my older brother Austin, his face also streaked with mud and fear, clutched his own spear while Papa raised his Browning automatic rifle to his shoulder. This was the first time I'd been allowed to accompany them into the bush to hunt, and I dared not show my terror. The boar looked huge with an elongated snout protruding from small dark eyes. It was as long as a man is tall and weighed as much as a yearling calf.

Despite their size, the giant forest hogs were surprisingly fast and would charge when threatened. I'd been chased by a group of them once before when I was with Papa. This animal's thick, curved tusks looked like daggers ready to skewer me at any moment.

Trying to keep from trembling, I stood my ground.

"Be ready, Kono," Austin whispered. For a moment, I thought he was teasing me, but one glance at his face convinced me otherwise. He lifted his spear higher. Papa sighted down the barrel of the rifle. If the first shot was clean, Papa had told us, the hog would only be wounded and become even more dangerous. I held my breath as Papa squeezed the trigger.

From just a few feet away, the noise was deafening. The bullet hit its mark in the neck just behind the creature's ear, and the giant hog let out a squeal. It didn't charge, but it didn't drop either, swaying as it stared at us with menacing eyes. Papa fired again. This time the big creature listed to one side with a grunt and flopped lifeless into the grass, slapping the ground like someone beating a wet blanket.

"Subhanallah!" My brother and I jumped up and down in excitement. I touched the amulet around my neck I'd been given as a younger child and breathed a silent prayer of thanks. *My first hog!*

After chopping down a nearby small tree to make a pole strong enough to carry the dead creature, we made our triumphant return to the village to butcher it. Later, I stepped into our hut drenched in sweat and animal blood. Mama asked me if I'd been scared facing down the giant boar.

"No. I was brave. Just like Austin and Papa."

Mama smiled, patiently listening to my lie, her eyes alight with laughter. She gently steered me back outdoors and directed me to stand on a large, flat rock. I held still long enough for her to bathe me with a jungle shower, gently pouring a pitcher of water over my head the way my grandmother once had, smiling and singing softly to me in her lyrical voice.

That evening, my mother and father took my brother and sisters and me to a large, open field at the edge of the rainforest. Building a fire, we skewered some of the boar meat on sharpened sticks and roasted it. The meat tasted sweet and savory and was so tender, it melted from our sticks into our mouths.

As it grew dark, I watched, fascinated, as the sparks flew upward into a cloud of smoke. Overhead, the blackness of the jungle night played backdrop to a thousand stars, their twinkling pinpricks of light like tiny beacons of a hope I'd never felt before. It was a hope for my future, a hope for something better, and a trust built on something greater than ourselves. Allah perhaps? What other hope could there be for the security of my family, my tribe, and my country, this one and only beautiful place on our planet?

During our meal, Papa, Austin, and I told our versions of what happened on the hunt. My own story was the most detailed and filled with exaggeration. But when I was finished, Mama smiled and hugged me around the neck, kissing me on the top of the head.

"You will be a brave and mighty warrior for Allah, my little Kono," she said softly.

"Yes, I will," I said, pushing away my fear with all of the bravado and certainty my young voice could muster.

Maybe Mama was right. Maybe I would.

CHAPTER THREE

New School

More than two years after the 9/11 attacks on America, fear about terrorism remained high throughout the world. For the United States in early 2004, the war in Iraq ground on with mixed success. The capture of former Iraqi dictator Saddam Hussein at the end of 2003 was tempered by weekly reports of new deaths among the American and Iraqi soldiers.

Around the time Beth and I and our children arrived back stateside from Ethiopia, the US Department of Homeland Security had begun tracking all foreign arrivals using new biometric identity technology as authorized under a recent law passed by Congress and signed by the president. It didn't take long for me to realize that beyond the trauma and horrific loss of life on 9/11, perhaps the greatest long-term impact of the terrorist attacks was the reintroduction of trauma into American culture, the likes of which may not have been felt since the attack on Pearl Harbor in 1941 or the assassinations of John F. Kennedy, Martin Luther King, and Robert Kennedy in the 1960s.

On a sunny morning a few days after our plane landed, I pulled into the driveway of Denver Christian School in Colorado. Next to me sat my daughter Abigail, ready to begin her first year of high school. Cars inched toward the school drop-off stop. Students flooded the entrance where several faculty and staff greeted the new arrivals with smiles, encouraging words, and high fives.

I brought our borrowed sedan to a halt behind the last car in line and turned to look at my daughter. "Scared?"

"Scared? Are you kidding? Terrified is more like it."

Of course she was. This was ninth grade and a brand-new school in a country and a culture from which she'd been absent for years. Like me standing in front of that giant forest boar at six years of age, she was about to enter a jungle.

"None of the kids here will remember me."

"Some might. And even if they don't, you're all in the same boat going into high school. They're probably just as frightened as you are."

"I want to go talk to the coaches this afternoon about my running."

"That's a great idea," I said. Abigail was a gifted athlete, a natural short-distance runner who'd never been able to develop her skills while we'd lived in Ethiopia.

We moved forward another car length.

"I heard you talking with Mom the other night about going back to Liberia."

"That's right."

"That makes me scared too, Daddy. I've heard it's dangerous. Why would you ever go back there?"

"You know Liberia is where your mom and I grew up and were married. It's where you were born. Your two grandmothers are there as well as your mom's father, my brothers and sisters, aunts and uncles who are still alive, and cousins who've survived the war."

"But didn't your family kick you out or something?"

"Yes, but that was a long time ago. Times change. People can change."

"Are people still fighting there?"

"Some, but I won't be going into any of those areas."

"Do we have the money to pay for you to travel there?"

"Mmmm. Now you're starting to sound like your mother." I smiled.

"I'm just worried, that's all."

"I understand. But I promise you I'm not about to do anything rash. God will protect me and you and all of our family. You just worry about your schoolwork and making new friends."

Our car reached the front of the line, and it was time for her to go.

"Good luck," I told her as she grabbed her backpack and started to climb out. "I'll be praying for you."

The thought occurred to me then that Christians in America often employ this phrase as a means of dismissing one another or assuring one another on the surface. But I wondered how many of them really understood just how sovereign God is and that praying to him on behalf of another can go far beyond simple mindless recitations, helping to unleash the power of God's Holy Spirit to work on their behalf.

Abigail stopped and turned back, leaning across the seat

to give me a peck on the check. "I love you, Daddy."

"I love you, too, Abby."

Before I knew it, she was gone, closing the car door behind her and offering me a small wave as she joined the stream of students entering the building.

CHAPTER FOUR

Outlast Them

My eight-year-old face flushed with embarrassment as I walked into the classroom at Kingsville Number 7 Elementary in Liberia for my first day of school. I was two years older and bigger than my classmates, and I was from a farming family. We were "contra pippo," or country people, and in Liberia at that time, country people didn't go to school.

I had to leave home to attend school here in Kingsville, which was more than a two day's walk from Balumah. I was only here because my adult cousin Mary Harrison and her husband Faryah Saar saw some spark of intelligence and mischievous curiosity in me and had pushed and lobbied for me to attend the school in their town and live with them during the school year.

Mary was a robust woman with an even bigger heart who lived with her husband Faryah. Kingsville was a more modern place than Balumah with luxuries like paved roads, electricity, and running water. Faryah had a good job working as a driver for the nearby Voice of America radio station that broadcasted

American-made programming all over Africa and into the Middle East.

Only years later did I appreciate the gift Mary and her husband gave to me. If it had been up to my parents, I would have been like most of the other children in our village at that time. I would never have attended school at all. But Mary was persistent, and my parents finally relented.

But on that first day, the rolled eyes and snickers of my classmates didn't make me feel like I'd received much of a gift. I tried to remember how protected I'd felt when Grandma Zinnah poured water over me in front of the whole village. I determined to outlast these other students and earn their respect.

There were more than two hundred of us crammed into one cinderblock building divided by thin partitions into classrooms. It wasn't much by Western standards, but it was all we knew. I was assigned to the first grade section. I knew I had to work hard because my parents wouldn't be pleased if I didn't do well. Like most native Liberian boys who'd been initiated into Poro, the secret bush society to which all village males belonged, I'd been given an additional name. Mine was Sumo, meaning big and powerful boy. Along with my size, I soon realized I was able to learn at a faster pace than my classmates, so it wasn't long before I felt much better about being in school.

I learned many things at Kingsville Elementary over the next four years. I learned how to read and write and how to do math. Number 7 Township was on the edge of the massive Firestone rubber plantation. The plantation was one of our country's most valuable natural resources. The American Firestone Corporation owned the property, and many

Americans lived and worked there, managing the native workers.

Rubber trees required tapping and draining by hand, similar in some ways to the way maple syrup is tapped from trees in North America. In between visits back home to work on the farm, I was exposed to many things I'd never seen before. Many of the Americans lived in big houses with swimming pools and other amenities. There was even a golf course.

Despite the injustice and inequities, Liberia during this time was mostly peaceful, and parts of the country were prospering. The Americans had a lot to do with that. Big American companies like Chase Manhattan, Pan American, and Firestone were making a huge impact in Liberia back then. America's history with my country ran deep. Firestone in particular had made a major investment in Liberia since the 1920s, owning and running the nearly three-thousand-square-mile Firestone rubber plantation from which much of the world's rubber was extracted. Most of the rubber needed to help America and its allies win WWII had come from Liberia.

In school, we learned about early American historical figures such as George Washington and Thomas Jefferson. We learned how Liberia had come into being as a result of freed black slaves returning from America to found a new nation in Africa. We learned that our Liberian capital of Monrovia was named after American President James Monroe, who had helped to sponsor such a movement.

We also learned that America was predominantly a Christian nation, which was not consistent with my Islamic upbringing but was in accord with the majority of Liberians. Maybe that's why people became Christians, I remember thinking, to get money and food and things like cars, nice clothes, and other things I'd only read about in books.

I also remember wondering even at that early age if there might be something more to this Jesus of Nazareth person than I'd heard about from my Muslim family and our imam.

***

By age twelve, I was ready for the fifth grade, and my cousin Mary transferred me into a larger school at Careysburg, a town only forty miles outside of Monrovia. Many people traveled back and forth between there and the capital, including foreigners, or "different-different people" as we liked to say in Liberia. For the first time, I was also in a class with many Americo-Liberian students, who were children of Liberia's ruling class.

"You're from what village?" they'd demand. "Balumah? Where's that?"

It was not my first and would not be my last experience of feeling different and out of place. About this time, I mostly stopped listening to Mary and her husband. I was old enough by then to begin making good money caddying at the golf course where the Americans played. I had also started working odd jobs and in the fields.

I began getting into fights at school as well. Being doubly discriminated against—first because I was a native Liberian with darker skin than the Americo-Liberians and secondly because I was from the Muslim minority—fueled my frustration. I always seemed to be getting into some sort of trouble.

Finally, during recess one day, the principal at Careysburg, Ms. Gouwa, summoned me into her office. I sat outside her door in the hallway as I waited to be called into the office, wishing I was out on the soccer field with the other students. On the hallway wall, someone had hung what was supposed to be an inspirational poster. It showed a beautiful photo of a colorful sunset over a dark ocean. A caption underneath proclaimed, "Never give up hope."

The poster failed to inspire me. In fact, I felt irritated at whoever had put it there. What hope did I, a native Liberian, have in our culture? I was just a "country person" who in the eyes of those with money and connections was doomed to be relegated to a second-class citizenship, consigned to fewer opportunities and even outright oppression.

What especially made no sense to me was an entry in one of my social studies textbooks about the American civil rights movement and the fight for equal rights for blacks then going on in the United States. But my Americo-Liberian oppressors weren't white people. They were descendants of former slaves. They'd never made up more than a small fraction of Liberia's overall population. Yet these descendants of former slaves had been able with their better resources, education, and connections to rule over our country, all but enslaving the rest of us, ever since Liberia had officially been founded as a nation more than a century earlier.

I didn't really understand all of the historical and social particulars of this oppression as I sat there outside Ms. Gouwa's office. But I felt its effects every day.

"Tony Weedor, you may come in now." Ms. Gouwa was a diminutive woman with a commanding voice. Seated behind her desk with a pair of reading glasses dangling from her neck, she took stock of me as I entered. "Take a seat, please."

The two student chairs in her office were made of metal and hard plastic. I folded my growing frame into one of them.

Though I'd already surpassed Ms. Gouwa in physical stature, there was no question as to who held the authority and power here.

We talked about my latest infraction, a fight between me and an Americo-Liberian boy on the playground. The other boy had to be sent home with a swollen black eye. His parents had contacted the school.

Did I have a good excuse? Not really. The slight against me was minor in the scheme of things. How could I explain my boiling-over anger to Ms. Gouwa, a good woman who had seen enough potential in me to give me several chances to redeem myself despite my self-destructive behavior?

To Ms. Gouwa, I must have seemed unrepentant. When offered the opportunity to explain myself, I sat mute in my chair.

After a prolonged silence, the principal finally shook her head. "I don't know what to do with you, young man. You are wasting your life."

Back at my Cousin Mary's house, I wasn't getting along well with her or her husband, Faryah, either. They'd tried to place restrictions on me to help me stay in school, but I wasn't listening. Increasingly, I began skipping school, sneaking out to earn money or find trouble. I also snuck out at night to run with a pack of delinquent boys.

That evening, Mary called me into the small kitchen of her house. The look of pain and disappointment on her face was palpable as she told me the principal had called her and was planning to expel me. I stared at the floor, again unable to speak. For Faryah and Mary, I'd apparently used up all of my excuses and chances to change. Mary especially had done so much to help give me an educational foundation, and in return I'd betrayed her trust.

I clenched my fingers in pent-up frustration as Mary went on to explain that, since I was no longer listening to her and Faryah, she was taking me back home to live with my parents.

***

Years later, I would come to understand that my anger was a form of covering up for my fears. As a teen, I also seemed to have developed a knack for igniting rage within my father. My refusal to accept at face value everything I was told must have seemed like disrespect to him. My pointed questions and interest in reading might have also seemed like a threat to his authority.

I was now old enough to be given more responsibility when it came to family chores and work responsibilities. One day, we were outside our hut in the village. Too busy with friends, I'd forgotten to complete some vital task on the farm, and my father called me to account for this failure. I was trying to make excuses, which only served to heighten his anger.

Mama could get angry too, but she was generally more easy-going, always singing songs, usually in Belle or English but sometimes lilting into Mandingo, always getting along with people. My father was in many respects the opposite of Mama. Stern and often taciturn, he would not stand for any type of rebellion or anything he perceived as laziness or negligence, all of which he considered an affront to the family and to Allah.

Honed by years of military training and discipline, he flexed his muscles as he confronted me about my excuses and failure to do my work. A vein on the side of his head began to throb. Part of me wanted to run, but where could I go? Out of desperation, I said something I shouldn't have, trivializing the task I'd been given, questioning its validity, and even going so far as to suggest his entire farm was a waste of time.

My father rocked back on his heels like a volcano waiting to explode. For a moment, I thought I'd gotten away with my smart remark. Then without a word, my father turned and walked away from me, moving slowly across our muddy lawn like a leopard stalking its prey. As he bent down to pick something up from a stack of farming tools, I had a bad feeling something horrible was coming. What that was became clear when he turned back toward me with a large wooden pestle used for pounding and grinding grain.

He stalked toward me, gripping the handle with the pestle end held upward like a club—or an American baseball bat. His face had gone blank, and I wondered if this was the kind of face he'd worn while fighting in the Liberian Army years before. Even though I was big enough to defend myself, I knew I was still no match for him in a fight.

But before he could swing the club, Mama stepped in between us. Powerful in her own way, she demanded that my father put the club down. My father was having none of it. Pivoting, he turned his rage on her. Before either of us realized what was happening, he'd swung the pestle down forcefully across her back.

Mama slumped to the ground. I rushed in to defend her, but she held up her hand to stop me. My father raised the club again, but then he stopped. He stood there for a moment without a word, glaring back and forth between the two of us. Then he looked down at Mama shaking at his feet. He flexed his shoulders and twisted his neck as though the brief spasm of violence had for now at least satisfied some deep inner demon. His eyes glared into mine.

"You aren't worth it!" he said, spitting on the ground. Tossing the club back where'd he'd found it, he turned and walked away.

***

With my fourteenth birthday approaching, I must have understood I needed something else to help me overcome my own fears. With nowhere else to turn, I reached back, ironically, to my parents' teaching on Islam. To be accepted as a good Muslim, all I needed to do was submit. That sounded simple enough to me. Still, I didn't feel satisfied. I began to listen more closely and to pay closer attention to our Islamic practices, tribal traditions, and the dark mysticism of bush magic.

Maybe my heightened interest in my parents' religion was a subtle form of rebellion against the prejudices and injustices of the majority Liberian culture, which was almost uniformly Christian. Or rather, as I would eventually come to understand, our culture was dominated by a nominal or superficial form of Christianity espoused by the country's ruling elite—much as their ancestors had seen their slave masters in America going through the motions of superficial Christian religiosity more than a century before.

Without a genuine faith and personal relationship with a living God through Jesus Christ, any religion can be used to commit injustice and exploit others; it's happened too often throughout history to look away.

Whatever the reasons for my change of heart, my parents

were pleased with my deepening interest in Islam—though not necessarily with my constant questions. It was an unsettled time. I went back and forth between town and the farm, going to school only intermittently. Though I continued to score well on academic tests, I often felt sullen. My father's voice still echoed in my ears, helping to reinforce my shame. When I was older, I would come to realize my father's anger wasn't just about him. He was only one small part of a much larger culture in which appearance and reality were often two very different things.

I was working outside our hut late one afternoon when Mama's brother and his wife, Uncle Tommy and Sarta Davis, appeared. Breaking into a smile, I ran to greet them. I'd always enjoyed seeing Tommy and Sarta. They seemed so happy and full of life.

Mama also came out of the hut to greet them. "I didn't know you were coming. We would have been better prepared."

"We are so sorry for not sending word," Uncle Tommy replied. "But we have something important to talk to you about, and it just can't wait."

"Of course."

"It's about Tony."

"Oh. Please come in." Mama turned to me. "Tony, you go finish planting that row of corn. It needs to be done before dark."

Naturally, I had no interest in corn since I was burning with curiosity about what Uncle Tommy had to say, so I pretended to be planting while trying to keep an ear out for what they were discussing.

Uncle Tommy worked at the prestigious United Pentecostal School in Bomi Hills. United Pentecostal was a higher caliber school institution. The students there were both native and

Americo-Liberian, and they had excellent sports and other programs.

After the adults all went inside, I tiptoed around back to see if I could hear the conversation. I listened as my uncle told my mother there had recently been some changes at United Pentecostal and that he thought he might be able to help me gain entrance to the school. The Tolbert government in Monrovia was apparently coming under international pressure to open up more educational opportunities to native Liberians. Because I was athletic and had also done very well in school, I seemed to fit the bill perfectly. Just as before when I'd lived with Cousin Mary and her husband during the school year, Uncle Tommy was offering to let me live with him and Sarta while I went to school in Bomi Hills.

I could hardly believe my ears. Someone in Kingsville had told me Bomi was home to the Liberian Mining Company. Like Kingsville, there were paved roads, electricity, and the like, but apparently Bomi was even more advanced. Mama thanked Uncle Tommy for coming and for the opportunity, but said she feared that the Americo-Liberian students at such a prestigious school would persecute me because I was a native Liberian and a Muslim.

Uncle Tommy assured her that wouldn't be the case. Then Mama said she would need to discuss his kind offer with my father. I could tell she was wrestling with what was best for me—torn between what she wanted and her love for me.

For Mama, there were many advantages in keeping me at home. No one from our family had ever progressed very far in school, let alone a school like United Pentecostal. But Uncle Tommy and Aunt Sarta were very persuasive. As the conversation wound down, Mama seemed to be warming to the idea.

CHAPTER FIVE

State of the Union

During the first few weeks after our return to Denver in 2004, Beth and I busied ourselves setting up house and making sure our children were settling into their schools. I went to work teaching missionaries, visiting and speaking in churches to raise support for our continued ministry, and fielding dozens of questions about Muslims and how we as Christians are called to love them and serve among them as witnesses of the gospel.

On January 20, we all sat down to watch US President George W. Bush deliver his 2004 State of the Union Address on television. Bush spent much of his address talking about the war on terror and defending his foreign policy, in particular his decision to order the invasion of Iraq. He also spoke about a number of domestic issues, including immigration, referring again to his proposal to create a temporary worker program for illegal foreign migrants that would "preserve a path to citizenship … for those who respect the law, while bringing millions of hardworking men and women out from the shadows of American life."

I couldn't help but reflect about how my past was in many ways an exact reversal of the type of immigrant disparity Bush was describing. Growing up as a native black Liberian before 1980, I had essentially been forced to live in the shadows of Liberian life, even though only a small minority of other blacks were oppressing my people. What did my experience growing up in Liberia have to say about racism, slavery, and oppression? Maybe, at its core, the history of slavery wasn't really about racism but about a problem in the human heart.

CHAPTER SIX

The Way the Servants Go In

I got a second chance at schooling when United Pentecostal (UP) offered me a place in their sixth grade class. My parents seemed wary but—perhaps thankful to be temporarily rid of my rebellious spirit—they let me go.

School wasn't the only thing on my agenda. In addition to my studies, my feet were fast and served me well on the soccer field. Soccer was our country's major sport, and Bomi Hills had far better teams than I was used to, the team from UP being no exception. I learned some of the finer points of the game—for instance, to turn and follow a teammate's pass to me with my body between the defender and the ball in order to gain a step or two advantage.

At UP, my eyes were further opened to a different class of Liberians. Most UP students of Americo-Liberian birth came from stable homes where the lack of money and opportunity and the constant struggle for survival were not a constant reality. They had a relaxed, easy way about themselves. I made a number of friends, but as much as I tried to blend in, I always stood out because most Americo-Liberians had lighter complexions than my native black skin.

Did I feel discriminated against because I was a native Liberian? Not overtly from most of the friends I made. But the simple answer was yes. I couldn't help but feel the stares and insidious prejudice of assumptions made by some that I wasn't as smart as most of them because of my heritage.

Instead of confronting my hurt and fears, I inched further into carving out my Muslim identity. I was older than many of my classmates and would disappear into an empty room at different times of the day to pray. I also began asking more questions in class about the obvious disparities and inequities in our culture.

Near the end of the school year, I was lucky enough to be chosen to play on a club soccer team with a number of skilled Americo players, a couple of whom would soon become my friends. Ben Collins played for the national team and would go on to receive a scholarship to play college soccer in America. Montgomery Scott would later play with me in a semipro league, then play soccer professionally in Liberia.

Ben was a grade ahead of me, though we were the same age. Affable and a serious athlete and student, he was also a little rebellious like me. The day he invited me to visit his house after practice, I was thrilled but also a little scared and unsure what to expect. I told him I shouldn't go.

"Don't worry, Tony, everything will be okay," Ben insisted.

"Are you sure? What if your parents see me?"

"It'll be fine. I'll sneak you in the back door."

"They'll ground you."

"No, they won't. They're too busy with their own stuff. Besides, they'll never even know you are there."

Americo-Liberians controlled much of the economy and virtually all positions of power in Liberia. Ben's father was an important government official. Older Americo-Liberians treated me differently because they knew from my family name and darker skin I was not one of them. They considered native Liberians lazy, dull, and uneducated.

Despite my apprehension, Ben and I left soccer practice together and headed off in the direction of the more prosperous side of town. His house was about a fifteen-minute walk from the soccer field. I remember throwing stones along the way, joking and smiling with Ben, until we turned the corner on the street where he lived.

I stopped for a moment and stared at the large homes and green lawns. I could feel my heart drumming in my chest. Uncle Tommy and Aunt Sarta had a dwelling that was much nicer than our hut back in Balumah, but their house was nothing compared to the homes I saw here. There were flowers and picket fences. A couple of driveways had cars in them. A gardener was spraying water from a hose onto rich grass. It even smelled better than the Liberia I knew.

Where were all the goats, chickens, and cattle? Here there only seemed to be peace and prosperity. A few of Ben's neighbors were seated on their porches or working in their yards. I peered over my shoulder from time to time, ready to run if someone objected to my presence, but no one appeared to be paying us any mind as we walked along. At one point, I spotted a gardener who looked native like myself, but he was too attentive to his work to pay us any attention. Maybe the neighbors assumed that I too was just part of the hired help.

"Relax, Tony. You're my friend." Ben smiled, looking fully at ease as if I'd made this walk with him several times before.

We strode up to his house, a huge brick Victorian, and cut into a narrow lane between the dwelling and an adjoining brick wall.

"This is the way the servants go in," Ben said.

"You have servants?"

"Yes, dummy. What'd you expect? Actually, there are only two. Elsa, our cook, and Roberts, who's kind of a driver and handyman. But by this time, they've both gone home for the day."

"You have a car, too?"

"Yeah. The government gives my dad one. It's big and black. Some kind of German model."

We walked around to the back of the house. A huge porch ascended to the main floor of the house, while a side door with a real glass window led down to a lower level. Ben motioned for me to follow him. "This is where we go in."

Passing the porch, I glanced through the glass at a pair of rocking chairs, a wicker couch, and a strange-looking wooden seat suspended from a couple of chains attached to the porch ceiling.

"What's that?" I asked, pointing at the hanging wooden seat.

"Haven't you ever seen a porch swing?"

I shook my head. "You mean like the swings for the younger kids on the playground at school."

"Something like that," he said.

Inside, the wonders continued. The house even had running water and real flush toilets. I was rather revolted by the thought of bathrooms inside a house in the same dwelling where people slept. "You actually go to the toilet inside the house?"

"Of course." Ben looked at me with amusement. "Don't worry, it's sanitary. Everything goes through some kind of pipe into the ground."

"Amazing."

He laughed. "You should try it some time."

"No thanks."

I was suddenly conscious of my shoes. Ben, like most of the other Americo players on the team, wore new cleats. His were black with white stripes made in France. I'd grown up playing soccer for the most part in my bare feet. But when I joined the team, someone had given me an old pair of all-black cleats that were a size too big for me. I'd been thrilled to have them, but now I looked down at them and noticed how shabby they were and how many mud stains they had on them.

"I shouldn't be here," I said.

"What? I've barely just started showing you around."

"I need to go. I don't want to get caught. My aunt and uncle will be angry if I don't come home on time."

"Really?"

"Yeah."

"Does my house make you uncomfortable?"

"I guess so."

Ben looked at me for a long moment. "Yeah, okay. I suppose you'd better go on home to your own place now."

Part of me would have liked to stay and play soccer and finish high school in Bomi. But after my visit to Ben's home and seeing firsthand the differences in how his family lived, I had too many questions. They were questions I realized I would not find the answers to there. I was big enough and strong enough now to begin earning money on my own, doing things like caddying and clearing brush with a machete. I'd also learned and seen enough to come to the realization there was a much bigger world to experience beyond my region of Liberia, and I wanted to try to figure out how I, a native Liberian and a Muslim, fit into it.

On the last day of school for that year, as I said my farewells to Ben and my other classmates, I took one last long look around. Maybe I understood somewhere deep within me that this would be the last time I'd ever attend United Pentecostal School.

***

That summer, I was back on my father's farm tilling soil by hand when I made the decision that I needed to leave home. I was old enough now, and I could see no future for me in the village or on the farm. I would go to Monrovia and begin making money and supporting myself.

Though I loved books and learning, I had to ask myself what I would do with a high school diploma while living in a rural village surrounded by a culture that would never offer me full opportunity because I was a native Liberian. If I had to swim upstream, I would go to the city. Let me work there and go to school on my own terms.

Mama cried when I told her I was moving out, but I think on some level she understood I needed to get out from under my father's thumb. As long as I remained a strong Muslim, she would be proud of me.

She asked where I would go. I told her I would stay for a time with relatives in Monrovia. My older sister MJ and her husband lived there with their children, and I had an older cousin, Joseph Weedor, who would let me live with him in the city.

When I told my father of my plans, he sat stony-faced, looking through me as if I were a ghost. "There's nothing but trouble for you in Monrovia," he said with a look of disgust on his face. But he made no move to stop me. Maybe he thought trouble would be good for me. After all, he'd traveled throughout Liberia. He'd been to the Congo as well while he'd served in the Army. He knew things I could never know unless I went and experienced them for myself.

I'd saved up some money. Now I set about gathering together the few pieces of clothing and belongings I would carry for my journey. I may have been young, but I wasn't naive.

I wasn't any different, I suppose, than a hundred million dreamers before me. I believed I could thrive away from my backward ancestral home in a place where electric lights and running water were not unheard of, and where paved roads came together with banks, restaurants, and hotels. In Monrovia, I'd been told, taxicabs ran back and forth from the city to the international airport. Massive ships plied the harbor of one of the largest deep water ports in the world. I wasn't exactly expecting a paradise of milk and honey, but anything had to be better than my life in Balumah and on the farm.

Three days later, I was seated on a bus heading into the capital city of Monrovia. This was no small feat, since Balumah was not like Kingsville or Bomi and far more isolated. To get to Monrovia from my native village, I'd had to hike for nearly two days across fields and along jungle trails to the nearest dirt road.

The bus was nearly full when I got on, but I found a seat near the front and looked around. An overweight driver perched over the wheel with the stub of a cigar clenched between his teeth. Behind him, an old man in dirt-worn shoes and a stained suit smiled from time to time at something the driver was saying under his breath. Farther back and across the aisle, a harried mother with her bright red sari robe draped over one shoulder was doing her best to correct her three small children, who were fighting over some kind of toy.

As the bus neared the city, I stared out the window in wide-eyed wonderment at the number of people and buildings and cars. I'd sent word ahead to my cousin Joseph, who'd agreed to meet me when I got off the bus.

Joseph and I were similar in age. His father was my father's brother, who was also a soldier. When the bus pulled into the station, Joseph stood there waiting for me, his demeanor reflecting the composure and self-discipline his military father had helped to create in him. It was a composure that would one day earn Joseph a spot in the elite Special Forces of the Liberian Army.

But for now, Joseph was still a young teen and student just like me, getting ready for high school and helping to support himself and his family by working various jobs. Like me, he'd been forced to grow up fast, but in a worldlier environment. He knew the city well—places you could go and places to avoid. More importantly, he knew where work could be found.

For a time, I relished my newfound freedom. I liked being on my own and living with someone closer to my own age. Joseph put me up in a tiny apartment where he lived with two other students and only one bed. Four of us were forced to squeeze onto the same hard mattress at night to try to get some sleep, which was not the best of circumstances, but it was all we had.

With Joseph's help, I was able to find odd jobs around the city. But I soon began to realize I would not be able to support myself alone in the city with only occasional work. I had to either find more permanent work or figure out how to make money another way.

All sorts of people lived and worked in Monrovia. There were people from all different backgrounds and tribes as well as many expatriates from America and other countries. But they all had more money than a country villager, which meant that they could afford to buy things. That gave me an idea. One night I showed up on my older sister Ma-Jangar's doorstep.

MJ, as we called her, greeted me warmly. "Where have you been, Tony? I'm so glad to see you."

"I've been working, and you know I've been staying with Joseph."

"Ah. But I've been waiting for you to come see me. Look at you—my little brother all grown up and working here in the city."

We caught up on each other's lives and family news. MJ asked how Mama and Papa were doing and how they felt about me leaving. She seemed to understand my need to get out from beneath my father's thumb—maybe even better than I understood it then myself.

Then I told her about my idea. "I have a business proposition for you, MJ."

"A business proposition?"

"Yes."

"What kind of nonsense is this?"

In my short time in Monrovia, I'd noticed how many street

venders were adolescent youth like myself, selling everything from fruit and nuts to drinks and small sundry items. Like a startup capitalistic army, they plied the various street corners and busy thoroughfares, anywhere large groups of people congregated, in order to turn a profit on their goods. I was intrigued by their sales and the potential to earn an honest living. Maybe Mama's merchant blood was making its presence felt in me.

There was only one problem. I didn't have the money to pay for the initial inventory or the display case I would need to begin selling. So I asked my sister to loan me twenty-five dollars.

"Twenty-five dollars?" MJ was incredulous. "What you need twenty-five dollars for?"

"I will pay you back. I need to invest in a sturdy tray to tie around my neck and some market goods to sell to passersby in the city."

"You mean, you want to become a street vendor?"

"Yes."

"Forget it, Tony. There are too many of them already."

"But I've seen lots of people buying things from them. I just have to learn some of their tricks, then I will outsell them. I will make enough to pay my way here in the city and to pay you back."

"What about school?"

"I am going to try to go back to school here, after I start making some money."

I could tell MJ was still tempted to squelch my dream in that moment, but she also seemed to recognize my determination. She looked at me for a long moment, then turned to her husband, who'd been sitting quietly listening from across the room. "What do you think?"

"Give the boy his money," he said with a wave of his hand. "He might make it. He's smart enough! And if he doesn't pay you back, we'll know where to find him."

MJ relented and loaned me the money.

***

Within a couple of days, I was standing on the corner outside the main bus station with my new "market" hanging neatly around my neck. This was a wooden display tray showing off an assortment of candies, fruit, nuts, hair combs, chewing gum, small cartons of juice, and bottles of soda. I made sure to be the first one out that morning. Though the sun was barely above the horizon and few people were out and about, I'd learned from the station manager that a large bus filled with overnight travelers would be arriving soon. They would undoubtedly be hungry and thirsty and in need of some of the things on my tray.

But no sooner had the bus pulled up to the curb when several other vendors appeared as if out of thin air. Their trays were worn, and their assortment of goods was not as varied or fresh as mine, but they pushed past me to different spots along the sidewalk and curb. They knew from experience exactly where to stand to catch the attention of the arriving passengers.

Two of them stopped to talk to me. They were several years younger than me—I guessed around ten—and they looked over my shiny new tray with admiring eyes. I managed to sell a couple of things to a man and woman who'd gotten off the bus together, but that was all. Many of the other vendors seemed to be doing a much brisker business. I studied them to see how they interacted with their customers.

Meanwhile, the two young boys sat idly by looking a little crestfallen, and I couldn't help but notice they'd sold nothing. It wasn't long before all the passengers were off the bus and had departed. The three of us were left seated next to one another on the curb, our market trays at our feet. They soon began telling me about Monrovia and what it was like to sell on the street.

"Here," one of them said. "Let me show you something."

He directed me to one side away from the curb and started showing me one of the items on his tray, an attractive piece of costume jewelry he described in elaborate detail. Then he glanced over my shoulder. "Okay, nice talking to you, Mr. Tony. We got to go."

Before I could react, he and the other boy took off running around the back of the bus and quickly disappeared from sight. But not before I heard them laughing to one another.

"He Belle. You see the way he talk?"

"Yeah, he got his face washed!"

Turning back, I looked down at my tray on the curb. To my horror, half of my inventory had disappeared! I picked up a stone and started to run after the two boys, but then I realized it was too late. They'd melted down an alleyway, and I had no idea where they'd gone. I muttered to myself, kicking the ground in frustration.

"Little thieves."

***

Getting my "face washed" may have been my first hard lesson about life on the streets, but it wasn't my last. Thankfully, I was a fast learner. I worked from dawn to dusk selling goods from my tray. Before long, I was earning good money.

By the end of summer, I had become an expert at navigating the boulevards, byways, and alleyways of Monrovia. I knew every major street corner and the times of day when they were busiest. I sold my goods up and down Broad Street and in the Duala and Waterside markets. I stood for hours in the heat with my tray outside the beautiful Hotel Africa with its lobby of hand-carved wood, selling goods to hotel patrons. I also positioned myself whenever I could at the turnaround in front of the luxury Ducor Hotel.

I learned to frequent the bus station when the buses arrived and the best places to stand. I also offered my wares outside soccer games at Tubman Stadium. I even went so far as Freeport and Tubman Boulevard to do my selling. Mama's teaching about money and her example as a Mandingo merchant had clearly taken root in me.

Occasionally, I saw from a distance the two younger boys who'd "washed my face," but I ignored them. I was too busy conducting my business. As my confidence grew, I began to notice things I'd never known about as a boy from a country village. I came to understand in more detail the dysfunctional order of things in my country and the underbelly of Americo-Liberian hypocrisy.

I watched how prostitutes filled the roadside bars at night. I saw how certain powerful Americo-Liberian men had open affairs with young native girls, and how children born out of wedlock to such unions only fueled the cycle of corruption and hypocrisy. Meanwhile, anger and bitterness among the native Liberians continued to smolder.

The Americo-Liberian minority remained firmly in control of Liberia politically and economically. When long-term Liberian President William Tubman died in 1971, his vice president, William Tolbert, succeeded him. Tolbert was a career bureaucrat and politician who had risen through the ranks of the country's House of Representatives. He'd begun working to appease the demands for more power-sharing with the indigenous peoples. In 1973, Tolbert also reinstated the long-abolished two-party system by allowing the formation of an opposition party. The Progressive Alliance of Liberia, known as PAL, was headed by an opposition leader named Gabriel Matthews.

But the pace of change was still too slow for many among the native Liberian majority. By the mid-1970s, when I arrived in Monrovia, the city was rapidly becoming a center of unrest with pockets of protest and public marches held every few days.

By now, I'd managed to pay my sister back all of her money, which made her glad. With my extra profits, I bought a portable transistor radio to listen to the BBC and ELWA news. I also determined I should go back to school. I figured I could attend classes in the morning and work as a street vendor after school until dark, when I would go back to Joseph's apartment to study.

On the first day of school that fall, I walked into Newport Middle School in Monrovia, one of the largest public schools in the city, and asked to enroll. The man there had me fill out some paperwork, which I did to the best of my ability. By the next day, I was sitting in a classroom with all the other students.

I made a number of friends that year in school but chose to

keep my street vending a secret. While public school students weren't wealthy like those of the private schools I'd attended, other students either held jobs or received enough money from their parents to afford new clothes and book bags. A street vender was among the lowest of professions, and I was embarrassed to have my new classmates know I was supporting myself in that way. But I kept at it, hoping I would never run into one of my classmates on the street.

Several months passed. I still lived with my cousin Joseph, though MJ had offered to let me move in with her. I was doing well in school but had grown weary of supporting myself on the street. As the school year drew to a close, the rainy season arrived in force, making it harder to sell my goods on the street.

Little did I know that the change of seasons would also mark a turn in my own life, propelling me forward in a way I hadn't foreseen.

CHAPTER SEVEN

Borrowed Umbrella

I was standing in the rain at a bus stop in Monrovia when a man who would change my life tapped me on the shoulder and asked to borrow my umbrella. I was still working as a street vendor while going to school. With goods to keep dry, I'd learned long ago that you always needed an umbrella during Liberia's monsoon season.

I turned to look at the man. He wore a business suit and tie, a far cry from my jeans and T-shirt. His complexion was lighter than mine, and his hair had minimal curl. I'd sold goods on the street to men who'd said they were from India and were here doing business in Liberia; this man looked a lot like them.

He appeared harmless, though I wondered why such a well-dressed man wouldn't possess his own umbrella. Maybe he was new to Monrovia and didn't understand the need for umbrellas.

"Sure," I said, handing him mine.

He thanked me and explained in perfect English how he'd

forgotten his own umbrella and didn't have time to go back for it, since he was running late for an important business meeting. It was starting to drizzle; he didn't want to get his suit wet. He asked me my name, and I told him. The bus was running late, so we stood there for a while. He asked me if I was in school or working, then further questioned me about my education. I summarized my schooling for him, leaving out the part about being kicked out of fifth grade.

He said his name was Kumar Chaugani. He was indeed from India and owned several businesses in Monrovia. Then he asked if I was looking for more work. I told him yes, always. Pulling a business card from his suit pocket, he handed it to me. When his bus finally arrived, he returned my umbrella. Glancing back over his shoulder as he boarded, he told me to give him a call sometime about a job.

A few days later, I did call Kumar. He invited me to meet with him at his office, which was at the back of the Rivoli Cinema, one of the businesses he owned. I entered through a side door that opened onto a back alley. The office was a small, humble room where Kumar sat behind a desk covered with stacks of paperwork.

He invited me to sit opposite him in a wooden chair.

"I wasn't sure you'd call," he said. "But you made a good first impression on me. Tell me a little more about yourself."

I told him all about growing up in Balumah, about my parents and brothers and sisters, about playing soccer, and about working on the farm. He seemed genuinely interested in my background as well as my willingness to move to the city and work hard selling on the street. I also told him how I had enrolled in Newport Middle School and planned to complete a high school degree, possibly even go to college. He seemed very pleased with this. I explained too how I'd been living with my cousin Joseph and about my sister and her husband and children, who also lived here in Monrovia. He seemed satisfied with all these things as well.

Kumar in turn explained that he had moved from India to Monrovia some years earlier and was doing well as a businessman. He planned to marry someday, but currently lived alone in a large house that he didn't use as much as he'd like, due to business obligations and travel. He was looking for a live-in caretaker to keep an eye on things when he wasn't there, someone reliable he could trust. Would this be something that might interest me?

Would it! It seemed like a dream come true.

Then he looked at me with a piercing gaze as he asked, "Are you reliable, Mr. Weedor?"

"Yes, sir, I am," I said.

"Can I trust you?"

"Yes, sir."

That seemed to settle it. He nodded. "Okay, then. I'm offering you the job. You may live in my house free of charge, but here are my terms: You must help care for and watch over the house as well as be available to do odd jobs and to fill in at the theater or my restaurant when necessary. You must also stay in school. If there is a conflict between work and school, you must always go to class. I am willing to trust you until proven otherwise. How does that sound to you?"

"That sounds amazing. May Allah reward your goodness."

"Right. Is it a deal then?"

"Yes, sir."

"Good. You may start moving your things in immediately." Kumar rose to his feet. I stood up too, and we shook hands.

Kumar's house was palatial to me. It had a second story and three different bedrooms. But the most amazing thing was Kumar's library, a beautifully maintained separate section of the main living space. He owned shelves full of books, many of which I'd never seen, let alone read before, and I was given access to all of them.

For the next few years, I would live full-time in this house in between occasional visits back home. I would read every book in Kumar's library. I would continue progressing in school and begin earning top grades while also playing soccer. I would learn many things while living with Kumar, including forging my adult identity in the crucible of what had become increasing unrest and resentment in the streets of Monrovia and across Liberia.

***

My commitment to Islam continued to grow as well during this time. I prayed religiously and studied the Quran as well as the traditions of the prophet Muhammad. Though not a Muslim himself, Kumar didn't object. I think he saw my increasingly strict beliefs as a good way of keeping his property safe and me out of teenage trouble.

In Balumah, my Uncle Sekou was still the local imam. As the nephew of the spiritual leader for the local Muslims, I was exposed to Islamic teaching growing up more than most of my peers. It's important to understand, however, that while the Islam I was taught followed the basic tenets of the prophet Muhammad, they differed considerably from the Islam practiced in other parts of the world.

I've already mentioned how most African Muslims mix in mystical and spiritual traditions, such as animism from their own tribal and cultural heritages. Only a fraction speak Arabic, so the majority are reciting Islamic prayers they've learned by rote. The degree to which an African Muslim adheres to Islam orthodoxy also varies by tribe and region. For example, I was taught to pray by rote five times a day, as required by the prophet Muhammad. But I also wore an amulet and bracelets typically used in the practice of voodoo, which I was taught would provide protection from evil spirits.

Shame went hand in hand with fear, playing a huge role in the Muslim tribal culture in which I grew up. I would be shamed for not practicing absolute submission to my parents or for failing to follow the militaristic spiritual disciplines of the prophet. Sickness or other bad things that happened were the work of demonic forces arrayed against a person as a result of their own actions or because someone else had placed a curse or hex on them.

Let me make clear my experience with Islam didn't feel bad at the time. Quite the contrary, I felt a superficial sense of security and familial safety in sharing these beliefs with countless others who watched out for each other and took care of each other. A good Muslim was expected to feed you or even give you money if you needed it.

But in the middle of the night, none of these Islamic or tribal spiritual practices could make my fears go away. They provided only temporary, superficial relief. So as I grew older, I decided to double down with Islam. By the time I entered ninth grade, I even began to change the way I dressed as my Muslim identity developed deeper roots. I worked hard to keep myself apart from unsavory practices and shield my eyes from unwholesome things, discovering a certain pride in this form of self-discipline.

As my interest in Islam increased, so did my interest in Christianity. This was not because I had any interest at all in becoming a Christian, but because Liberia's dominant religion beyond tribal animistic practices common to all native Liberians was Christianity—at least on the surface. I read parts of the Old Testament as well as New Testament accounts of Jesus Christ in order to be able to refute their teachings with my own Islamic beliefs. Some of these refutations I'd been taught by the imams from an early age, but I began studying more deeply so as to be able to argue effectively against Christian doctrines.

On the first day of school that year, I wore a serwal and tunic common among Muslim men. One of my soccer friends spotted me from across the courtyard. "Tony, is that you?"

"Yes."

"Nice outfit, my man."

"Thanks."

"Is it Belle?"

"Nah." I smiled. My friend and I were from different tribes. To most Liberians, as in much of the rest of Africa, tribe was more important than country. My mixed tribal heritage—a Belle father and Mandingo mother—sometimes made things difficult for me when it came to navigating society. I felt like I never quite belonged. Like most Liberian men, I identified most with my father's tribe. But the Belle was a small tribe, and I'd had to learn to assimilate and get along with people from a number of different tribes while living in Monrovia. I'd learned a number of different Liberian tribal languages as well.

"You know I'm Muslim, right?" I said.

"Oh, yeah, right! So is that the kind of outfit Muslims wear?"

"Sometimes."

My faith became increasingly political as well. I began regularly reading the newspaper and listening to the BBC. I gained a keener interest in learning about Liberia's history, especially the exploitation of native Liberians by Americo-Liberians under the auspices of a superficial Christianity practiced by nineteenth-century slaveholders in the American South. Since I was already better educated than most native Liberians, Islam also became a way for me to stand apart from the hypocrisy and injustices of the Americo-Liberian culture. With my mixture of beliefs mined from both tribal African and Islamic teachings, I stuck to my amulets and prayers.

At home one night, I talked over the tensions going on in Monrovia with Kumar. Kumar was a patient man and an intelligent businessman. He was also by nature a peacemaker, one who accepted others for who they were and did business with people of all stripes. He wasn't about to embroil himself in Liberian politics, especially since for years he'd found Monrovia a relatively calm place in which to thrive, compared with the rest of Africa. But he also read the newspapers and listened to the radio and could sense the building tensions.

"You need to be careful, Tony," he told me.

"You're right."

"You've done everything I've asked of you living here. You've watched over things and been a good and faithful worker. You've continued on in school. You don't want to jeopardize what you have or where you're going."

"I understand," I said. "But big change may be coming."

"Trouble between tribes?" he asked.

"That and more."

He looked past me at something on the wall, the expression on his face inscrutable. "Just watch yourself. I don't want anything to happen to my trusted assistant."

Although I didn't join the demonstrations in the streets, I was encouraged by my teachers during my first two years at Charlotte Talbot High School to join their own intellectual revolution against Americo-Liberian rule. Like me, many of my instructors were young and idealistic. A number had traveled to the United States for further education. Some had even been swept up in the cause of the civil rights movement there.

Liberia, my teachers taught, represented in many ways a dysfunctional shadow and close relative of the American South's own segregation and racial discrimination. They may very well have been right, but in the tumultuous social currents beginning to rip through Africa at that time, it was often hard to tell the difference between those who were truly seeking to reform such injustices and those who were out to exploit for their own gain all the anger and frustration over injustice.

In my high school classes, I learned that Liberia had been controlled for more than a century by a single political entity, the True Whigs, which was the political party tightly controlled by the small minority of Americo-Liberians. It had been the country's only real political force for generations, engineering the succession of every Liberian president since 1847 right up until President William Tubman, who had been in power from 1944 until his death in 1971. Having served as Chief Justice of the Supreme Court before being elected president, Tubman was known as the Father of Modern Liberia for helping to bring the country into the twentieth century. This included attracting significant foreign investment and modernizing the country's infrastructure. His handpicked successor and longtime vice president, William R. Tolbert, had followed Tubman into office, but he had big shoes to fill, since Tubman was still revered by many Liberians.

Meanwhile, America continued to be our country's longtime benefactor and ally. In order to ensure the continued flow of rubber from Liberia's Firestone plantation during WWII, the American military had constructed the country's main commercial shipping port, the huge Freeport of Monrovia, with its two breakwaters and artificial harbor. In June 1944, President William Tubman had even traveled to America with his predecessor, Edwin Barclay, at the invitation of Franklin D. Roosevelt, the first African heads of state to ever be hosted at the White House.

But Liberia's peace and prosperity relative to other developing African nations continued to mask a smoldering cauldron of resentment among native Liberians, who, due to divisions caused by tribal differences, had never been able to effectively organize; they'd been ruled over by the small minority of Americo-Liberians for more than a century. Despite promises and reforms over time—like grudgingly granting native Liberian property owners the right to vote—the country's leaders continued to crush any and all who opposed them. While the vast majority of Liberians lived in squalor, they couldn't help but stare in frustration and resentment at the growing prosperity that Americo-Liberians, and those who did their bidding, were enjoying. Every native Liberian had felt the sting of oppression in one form or another; especially those who'd attempted to organize against the country's ruling party and elite.

During my sophomore year of high school, unrest among indigenous Liberians in Monrovia, especially students at the University of Liberia, began building toward a boiling point. Many high school students like me were influenced by the activism and teachings of Gabriel Matthews, a former Foreign Service Officer in the Tolbert administration and founder of the Progressive Alliance of Liberia (PAL). Boima Fahnbulleh, a professor at the University of Liberia, was also very influential at the time. So was Dr. Togba-Nah Tipoteh, another university professor with a PhD in economics who headed a leftist political organization known as the Movement for Justice in Africa (MOJA) in which Fahnbulleh also take part.

All three of these academic leaders had received their college degrees in the United States, where they had been strongly influenced by America's civil rights movement. But another strong influence was the Marxist and socialist movements prevalent all over the developing world at that time, especially in the universities. After years of political and social injustice at the hands of an oppressive regime masquerading under the banner of democracy and capitalism, I and many other young Liberians became card-carrying socialists.

Two of my favorite teachers at Charlotte Talbot were Mrs. Momolu, my social studies teacher, and Ms. Ajuvan, my science teacher. After social studies class one day, Mrs. Momolu pulled me aside. "Weedor, I'd like to have a word with you."

I went and stood by the doorway while the other students filed out, towering over Mrs. Momolu, who was a good head shorter than I. But Mrs. Momolu wasn't intimidated by much of anything, and she certainly wasn't about to be intimidated by me. After the others disappeared, she strode up to me, grabbed me by the collar, and pulled my face close to hers to make sure she had my complete attention. "I noticed you weren't focusing too well in class today."

I said nothing.

"Weedor," she said. "You don't realize how much potential you have."

I continued to stare at her.

"You're a good athlete, and you're intelligent. You can easily make it through high school here without challenging yourself too much academically, but you're going to need to study more on your own if you really want to make something of yourself. It's no secret big things are about to happen in Liberia, and you can be a part of all that. You can go to college. Maybe even more."

I still didn't know what to say. Kumar and others believed in me, but no teacher had ever called out such a vision for me before.

"Think about it," she said, letting go of my collar. "Now you go on to soccer practice and keep yourself out of any trouble on the street."

I nodded and did as she said.

I spent a lot of time thinking about her words that day in the weeks and months to come. Little did any of us realize that a very big trouble was coming for me and for everyone else in Liberia. It was a change in the course of our nation's history perhaps none could have foreseen.

CHAPTER EIGHT

Finding Mama

As spring 2004 approached, I still wasn't sure what to do about tracking down my mother. We'd heard through acquaintances that Mama was still alive, but they didn't know where she was currently living, only that she was no longer in Balumah or the surrounding area.

In the wake of the wars, much of the country's population had been displaced. News reports out of Liberia indicated that a fragile ceasefire imposed by United Nations peacekeepers was still holding. Foreign troops operating under the UN flag had occupied Monrovia and were also taking control of most of the rest of the country. But travel to Liberia was still not advised by the US State Department, much less venturing too far outside the capital.

Communication was still very difficult, if not impossible. I had an uncle who last I'd known still had some high-level contacts in Monrovia, so I tried to get word to him through the American embassy. After a number of failed attempts, I finally managed to make contact with him by phone.

He informed me that Mama was living not far from him in a shantytown outside Monrovia. She was not in the best of health, and conditions were very bad there, he said. Terrible things had been done in the fighting, he warned me. He didn't sound at all encouraging about me attempting to make contact with Mama, let alone trying to visit her.

A bad connection soon forced our conversation to end, and I hung up feeling discouraged and depressed.

Nine Poles

I was in class at my high school on April 14, 1979, the day Gabriel Matthews and the PAL called for a peaceful public protest in Monrovia and a march on the Executive Mansion. The purpose of the march was to protest an unexpected government-mandated increase in the price of rice, which hurt the poorer Liberians above all.

What began as a small group of protestors soon swelled to a crowd of over fifteen thousand, many of them yelling and making threatening gestures. After so many years of peace, the Monrovian police were ill-prepared for such an event. President Tolbert and city officials panicked at such a spontaneous outburst of protest against their longtime rule, and orders were given to break up the gathering. Rock and bottle throwing ensued along with hand-to-hand fighting. Then desperate police officers began indiscriminately firing their guns at protestors.

From across the city, we could hear gunfire echoing like distant firecrackers through the open windows of our classroom. At first, our teachers warned us to stay in our seats. But after receiving some kind of message from the principal, they suddenly decided to close down the school and ordered us all to go home.

The rioting went on for more than twelve hours. By nightfall, fires from burning buildings could be seen all over Monrovia. Nearly fifty protestors were killed, and over five hundred were injured. Rumors spread throughout the city about out-of-control looting at the Center Supermarket on 12th Street, which turned out to be true.

Kumar begged me to stay inside, so I did, listening to reports about the rioting on local radio and eventually on the BBC. I don't remember sleeping that night. Something seemed to have changed in the atmosphere. An intense, vengeful anger was bubbling up out of a darkness in which it had lain dormant for more than a hundred years.

The next morning, windows in our neighborhood rattled as Guinean military helicopters—ordered in because Tolbert was friends with the president of Guinea—swooped in over the city bearing troops to help restore order. In all, over 150 stores had been looted, with a number completely destroyed. A few of the fires were still burning.

President Tolbert shut down the university, accusing the professors of fomenting unrest. Over the next few days, the existing order was restored and I eventually returned to my high school with my classmates. But the seeds had been sown for violent revolution, an upheaval none had ever dreamed of before.

As 1979 turned into 1980, the BBC news overflowed with stories from elsewhere in the world, in particular about the Iranian/American hostage crisis, in which radical Islamic students under the influence and direction of the Ayatollah Khomeini had seized the American Embassy in Tehran and was holding fifty-two American citizens hostage.

In Liberia, due to American and other international pressure after the bloodshed and political disasters of the rice riots the previous spring, the Tolbert administration had finally agreed to allow the formation of an opposition political party. Gabriel Matthews's organization, known as the Progressive Alliance of Liberia (PAL) was now officially recognized as the Progressive People's Party or PPP. These were exciting developments for me and many other young people, especially those of us among the "country people" who felt drawn to the cause of the PPP. Still, unrest and sporadic conflicts in the streets continued, and it was beginning to feel like too little too late.

Throughout the next few months, PPP, the Tolbert government, and MAJO engaged in a public war of words on radio, television, and at public rallies. Tolbert branded the opposition PPP and MAJO as socialist extremists bent on taking over Liberia. Eventually he had enough and decided to throw a number of his leading political opponents in jail, charging them with treason. Tolbert, who was also the chairman of the Organization for African Unity, was walking a fine line between his American and Western supporters and his propensity for tyrannical oppression of political opposition.

My junior year at Charlotte Tolbert Memorial Academy was rapidly drawing to a close. Tensions remained high as the one-year anniversary of the rice riots approached. On the morning of April 12, Kumar awakened me a little after 5 a.m. Turning on the light, I looked at him standing in the doorway.

His lips were drawn tight, his eyes filled with a haunting look of shock and fear.

"What's happening?"

"They're broadcasting on the national radio," he said. "Come and listen with me."

"Who's broadcasting?" Jumping out of bed, I wrestled into my clothes. From the other room, I could hear a voice I'd never heard before coming from Kumar's radio. "What's going on?"

"I'm not sure yet," Kumar said. He added that one of the neighbors had run over to wake him up and tell him to turn on the radio. The neighbor said something big was happening, and rumors had already begun to fly through our neighborhood, which was near the American Embassy. Across the city, the Executive Mansion was apparently under some sort of attack.

Another neighbor poked his head in our door to say that he'd heard President William Tolbert, successor to 137 years of despotic Americo-Liberian rule, might have been killed. Tolbert dead? I could hardly believe what I was hearing. Had native Liberians killed him?

Rubbing the sleep from my eyes, I tried to make sense of what was happening. Had PPP or MAJO somehow overthrown Tolbert's government? Who were these men with their strange voices on the radio? They said something about being soldiers, and they spoke in broken English, often lapsing into Krahn, one of Liberia's tribal languages.

I glanced at Kumar, who looked as dumbfounded as I. My employer and benefactor had much to lose. While he was a successful businessman, he was neither native Liberian nor Americo and was not considered a Liberian citizen. He was caught in the cultural crossfire.

Over the next few hours as the sun rose over Monrovia, no one seemed to know what was going on. It was a Saturday, so there was no school. On the radio, garbled voices could be heard proclaiming they'd killed "Pa," a reference to President Tolbert. More than once I caught a mention of someone named Samuel Doe. In the distance, we could hear sporadic gunfire and the sounds of big trucks moving. Everyone was afraid to go out.

Around 7 a.m., a more familiar, official-sounding voice came on the national radio. It was Gabriel Nimley, a well-known Monrovian radio and television broadcaster. He read the following announcement:

Today, April 12, Liberia's President and Chairman of the Organization of African Unity (OAU), Dr. William Richard Tolbert, Jr., has been assassinated in a coup staged by enlisted men of the Armed Forces of Liberia.

This proclamation was followed by a blast of music that included the Liberian national anthem: "All hail, Liberia, hail. All hail, Liberia, hail. This glorious land of liberty . . ."

The music was followed by more information about something called the People's Redemption Council and a person named Master Sergeant Samuel Doe, who was apparently the new man in charge. Who was Samuel Doe? Was someone playing a hoax?

I looked across the kitchen at Kumar. The two of us sat stunned, trying to make sense of what we were hearing. According to what I'd heard from Joseph and other relatives who'd been in the military, outside of the president's personal guard and a couple of well-trained brigades, most of the soldiers in the Liberian Army were not considered much of a threat. Unlike Tolbert and the Americo-Liberians, the soldiers were poorly paid and lived with their families in squalid conditions like most of the civilian population.

A short time later, we began to hear more gunfire, followed by singing, drumming, and chanting. Some fighting continued, but pockets of jubilation had also erupted throughout the city. Slowly it began to dawn on me that everything the man had said on the radio was true. A revolution was happening. We, the native peoples of Liberia, were finally taking our country back.

I didn't know quite what to feel. I resented the Americo-Liberians' oppressive rule, but I hadn't wanted it to end in bloodshed. I remembered one of my teachers talking about what might happen if the Americo-Liberians were ousted from power. He'd speculated about a struggle among various tribal groups for dominance, but I'd assumed he was talking about some sort of political struggle—not the kind of abrupt, violent upheaval we were now seeing.

Throughout the next hours and days, we learned more about the Samuel Doe who'd been mentioned on the radio. A member of the Krahn tribe serving in the Liberian Army, he had only recently been appointed to the rank of Master Sergeant. Recruiting a loyal group of enlisted Krahn soldiers, he had led them—dressed in painted tribal masks—in a bold, unbridled attack on the Executive Mansion. There they had killed a number of guards and brutally assassinated President Tolbert; they'd even disemboweled the president, known as "Pa" to many Liberians, in a tribal ritual believed to prevent a powerful witch doctor from coming back to life. Several others in the mansion, including members of Tolbert's personal security force, were also wounded or killed during the attack.

As Doe began to consolidate his power, most Liberian

army units deserted their posts and threw their loyalty behind him and his embryonic military government; sporadic fighting had begun to descend into chaos. Looting spread across the city, with even some of the soldiers taking part.

Throughout Liberia, Americo-Liberians, who the day before had been in control of the country, were suddenly forced into hiding and in many cases had to run for their lives. Americo-Liberian homes and properties were confiscated and ransacked. A curfew was imposed. But pillagers bent on wanton destruction continued to roam the streets, jubilant over what had happened but also seeking revenge for years of oppression.

For the time being, my school year had been suspended. I was happy we were free of Tolbert's Americo-Liberian government, but also worried and frightened at all the chaos and people out of control. Kumar was worried he would lose his theater and other businesses in the looting. I tried to reassure him that most people were only after Americo-Liberian property, but who really knew for sure?

***

On April 22, 1980, ten days after the assassination of President Tolbert, I was out in the street with dozens of others crowding around a small television set someone had set up. Like most everyone else in Monrovia that day, we were gathered to watch an execution on the beach where nine large poles had been erected in the sand.

Up the coastline from the city, the sun rose over the ocean like a dirty round fire in a hazy blue sky. In the streets near Barclay Barracks—the main military garrison in the shadow of Liberia's Executive Mansion—a horrible sense of anticipation filled the air as they prepared to transfer thirteen prisoners to the seashore. There with ocean waves breaking in the background, the thirteen men would be strapped to the poles buried in the beach, then shot by a firing squad. Radio and TV would be broadcasting the event live throughout the country.

The reason for the execution was a brief kangaroo court where Doe and his newly formed People's Redemption Council had given the order to summarily execute most of Tolbert's cabinet members and other high government officials for "corruption and crimes against the people."

Were all these men guilty of such heinous crimes that they deserved such swift punishment? In the rush of events, it didn't really matter. People thought we were taking back our country from our oppressors. Master Sergeant Doe wanted the former officials executed in order to complete the task, and he was now firmly in control.

Standing in the crowd on the street a few blocks from the beachfront with some of my fellow students, I knew more than most. One of my uncles had presided over the civilian panel that had considered treason and corruption charges against the most powerful surviving Americo members of Tolbert's cabinet. The panel had recommended only three be executed for their crimes and the others sentenced to prison. But Doe had apparently overruled their decision. He had decided that all thirteen leading members of Tolbert's government must be executed immediately.

Maybe Doe feared these influential men could challenge his power. Maybe he was afraid of their superior education. Doe had already suspended the constitution, and the new self-declared president had simply used my uncle's civilian panel, despite its good intentions, as political cover for his new military government to do as they pleased.

Most of us would only become aware of these details later, however. Very few stopped to process what was actually happening. My young native Liberian friends and I were jubilant. All we cared about was that the many generations of Americo rule and oppression were finally at an end. The executions symbolized the beginning of a new era, one we hoped would represent a bright future for all Liberians. A celebratory mood filled the streets of the capital with singing, dancing, and the sound of sporadic shots being fired into the air.

Doe invited the international media to cover the mass execution. A little after noon, we watched as the Tolbert officials were marched onto the beach and each bound around the waist to their poles. Because there were only nine poles, four of the thirteen had to watch the execution of their colleagues as they waited their own turn.

None put up any resistance, apparently resigned by this point to their fate. It was hard at first to tell exactly what was going on. The firing squad looked undisciplined. Some of the soldiers even appeared to have been drinking. A surreal air of chaos seemed to permeate the beautiful beachfront as the crowd cheered and jeered. Some of the soldiers, either out of nervousness or lack of training, appeared to have difficulty loading their weapons or needed help from the officers in charge.

As happy as I felt about the change in government, I couldn't help but wonder about the horror I was witnessing and the stability of men now running our country. Would they really give us a new government by the people as they'd promised in their proclamations?

As the hail of gunfire began, the men slumped one by one in death against their poles. Around me, the crowd watching the TV started to shout and dance in joy. Someone had brought out a tape recorder with audio speakers, and it began blasting a recording of the national anthem.

I was twenty years old. I was soon to graduate from high school and take the entrance exam for the University of Liberia. With the Americo-Liberians ousted from power, a brighter future now seemed to loom before me. Like the rest of the city, I was suddenly swept up in the release of pent-up anger and frustration, the overheated euphoria of revenge mixed with the vague hope that things would soon be better; so I joined in the dancing and shouting with the crowds, jumping up and down and singing native tribal songs.

***

The schools reopened later that summer. I was playing soccer with friends on the field behind our school when we noticed a large group of workers climb out of a small convoy of trucks. They headed toward the main building, which was the largest public high school in Monrovia at the time. Some carried paintbrushes. Others had carpenter's tools, ladders, and sheets of plywood.

I stopped playing for a moment to watch them, wondering what was going on.

"Why are you stopping, Tony?" one of my friends shouted.

I pointed at the men.

"Haven't you heard, Man? They changed the name of our school."

Our school had long been named Charlotte High School

after former President William Tubman's daughter Charlotte. Since the April coup, however, Monrovia had been stewing in a mixture of hope and turmoil as the Doe regime tightened its grip on everything, including the educational system. Apparently in an effort to wipe out any memory of Americo-Liberian rule, they'd decided to rename our school Monrovia Central High.

The new name felt strange to me at first, like someone was ripping out an important part of our history and my identity; but, like a lot of other things, I supposed I would have to get used to it.

By now, most Americo-Liberians had fled Monrovia. Many had gone into hiding in other countries or the interior of Liberia. Thankfully, my own living situation remained stable. Kumar had been fortunate. His businesses had survived the transition to the Doe government, so I was still able to live with and work for him while I finished high school.

I wasn't sure if my educational background was strong enough to gain acceptance to college, but I applied to the University of Liberia anyway and took the required entrance exam. I remember standing in the living room of Kumar's house when I received my score.

"Open the envelope," Kumar said.

"I can't."

"C'mon! Go ahead. Be brave."

Undoing the seal, I folded open the paper with my test score to take a peek, then quickly folded it shut again.

"Well?" Kumar asked. "What is it?"

My face broke out in a wide grin. "I passed!"

He smiled broadly and clapped me on the back. "You did it! Congratulations!"

My mood remained buoyant for the rest of that school year. Before I knew it, the school year had ended. All too soon, I found myself marching down the aisle with my classmates for our high school graduation. No one from my village had ever graduated from high school before. It was a proud and joyous moment as I looked out over the assembled crowd in my cap and gown. Ceremonies mean a lot in Liberia, and this day would be no exception. I received my diploma with honors. Then I was presented an award for leadership. As I received it, I drank in the applause of my friends, family, and the assembled crowd.

Afterwards, my family and friends headed with me to one of Kumar's restaurants where we celebrated with singing, dancing, wonderful food, speeches I can no longer remember, and more gifts and praise. The celebration lasted far into the night, and I felt buoyant. I was so excited about college and my future.

I had no way of knowing God had in mind a major detour for me, one that would again alter the entire trajectory of my life.

***

One rainy summer morning a few weeks after my high school graduation, I awoke feeling a cold tremor of discomfort. *Maybe it's something I ate*, I thought.

But it wasn't.

Climbing out of bed, I grew lightheaded and nearly collapsed. I was supposed to be playing soccer with friends that afternoon if the skies cleared. Attempting to shake off whatever was bothering me, I tried doing some pushups on the floor, but that only made me grow dizzier. I climbed back in bed and started shivering; soon my body was bathed in sweat.

Okay, a fever. I'd dealt with this kind of thing before. I stumbled out of bed and drank some water before lying back down. Maybe I'd been working too hard. Maybe all I needed was rest. I went back to asleep, assuming the sickness would pass.

But it didn't go away; my illness grew worse. I felt weaker and weaker as the day went along. I couldn't take any nourishment. I managed to choke down a couple of aspirin, but nothing seemed to help. By midafternoon, I could barely lift my head up for Kumar or whoever else might be there to give me sips of water.

Later that evening, I opened my eyes and stared at the ceiling, unable to move a muscle. I vaguely remember Kumar coming to check on me. He was speaking softly and placed a cool cloth on my forehead. He tried to get me to drink some more, but I could barely lift my head, and most of the liquid dribbled down the side of my cheek.

Throughout the long night, I drifted in and out of an uneasy sleep. Heat seemed to radiate through my body like it was on fire. By morning, or what I thought might be morning, I'd lost all track of time. Others seemed to move in and out of the room, though I was only vaguely aware of their presence. The tone of their voices as well as Kumar's sounded grave. What was wrong with me? Was I dying?

I found out later that a nurse was called to come to the house. But it took her some time to arrive, and when she finally did, she just checked my symptoms and listened to my heart with her stethoscope before shaking her head. The line between life and death could be so fragile in our country. Few Liberians trusted Western hospitals, even in Monrovia, and no one seemed to know what was wrong with me.

I'm told I slipped into unconsciousness and became unresponsive. Kumar and others around me began to prepare for my imminent death. It was determined that if I was going to die, it would be best for me to be buried at home in my village with my family. But of course there were still no paved roads leading to Balumah, only worn jungle paths. The only relatively fast connection with the outside world was the municipal airstrip that had been hacked out of a field and was flat enough and usually dry enough for a small plane to land.

Joseph's father used his military connections to secure a small aircraft. At the airport outside Monrovia, Joseph and a few others carried me on a stretcher to the plane. Kumar was there, too. It must have felt like a sad way to see me, a healthy young man, head off to die. Later Kumar told me none of them ever expected to see me again.

CHAPTER TEN

Madrid Bombing

I was at home in Denver with Beth on the morning of Thursday, March 11, 2004, when news broke about the worst Islamist attack in European history. Ten bombs packed with nails had exploded on packed commuter trains at four different rail stations in Madrid, Spain. One hundred ninety-three people died. Almost two thousand were maimed or injured. The authorities would soon discover the bombs had been detonated remotely by using cell phones.

Speculation about who was responsible ran rampant. A group linked to Al-Qaida first claimed credit. Then a number of experts began pointing to the Spanish Basque separatist group known as ETA. But according to a later report in the UK *Guardian*:

> The police investigation and subsequent trial uncovered no evidence of a link to Eta. The bombings were carried out by a group of young men, mostly from north Africa, who were, according to prosecutors, inspired by a tract on an al-Qaida-affiliated website that called for attacks on Spain. The tract called for "two or three attacks ... to

exploit the coming general elections in Spain in March 2004", saying that they would ensure the "victory of the Socialist party and the withdrawal of Spanish forces [from Iraq].

For many in America, the impact of the Madrid attack, along with other Islamist attacks in Iraq and elsewhere, further stoked a cloud of fear that hovered over the West. I continued to be flooded with questions from Christians about Islam, and as the war on terror intensified, I couldn't help but be reminded of the dark times of upheaval, chaos, and murder I'd lived through in Liberia. More importantly, I couldn't help but think back to the time and the circumstances that would bring me my own deliverance from fear.

CHAPTER ELEVEN

Face Yourself

Sometime during the flight home, I remember briefly opening my eyes. The small plane droned tunelessly as it soared over the jungle. What was going on? Was this heaven? Floating through the sky, barely clinging to life, I felt as though reality had turned in on itself. Then I drifted back into unconsciousness.

As I later learned, the entire village came out to greet the plane when the wheels touched down on the narrow dirt runway. Everyone was crying. My parents were there, my mother tearfully hugging me while my father and Uncle Sekou chanted prayers over my unconscious form. The village witch doctor arrived, and soon I was sprinkled with the blood of a dead goat, immersed in counter curses, draped in talismans and herbs, and given potions to help ward off whatever demons had invaded my body.

I remember none of this, of course, and it doesn't really matter because nothing seemed to work. I was conscious only for brief periods over the next couple of days, and when I was, I felt sicker than ever. One thing I do remember was crying out weakly in my dreams to Allah for help. But help never came.

Arrangements were apparently already under way for my Islamic funeral. There was really nothing else to be done since no one here trusted Western medicine, clinics, doctors, or hospitals. In any case, there were few if any of these within a hundred miles. For centuries, the people in my part of Liberia had relied, not on science or even monotheistic religions for hope and healing, but on ancient tribal curses, bush devils, and other spirits, all part of the folk Islam I talked about earlier. Even as a small child, I was taught this through example. Demons and evil spirits were to be feared because they possessed some supernatural power humans were mostly powerless against. When sickness appeared in an otherwise healthy person, this was considered to be the result of the person's own evil action or someone else's curse. Everyone was scared—not just for me but for themselves. No one knew who might have cursed me or how.

For the next few days, I went through a period of hallucination and had no idea where I was. Was I still alive or in some netherworld? As I recall, it seemed like a little of both. I could see the walls of the hut where I'd grown up and spent so much of my childhood. I could sense my parents nearby, especially my mother.

But I no longer inhabited my body. Sometimes I moved around inside of the hut, and sometimes I was outside instead, enveloped in a blanket of heat and humidity like some sort of cocoon and floating through the rainforest. Elephants, wild monkeys, leopards, and even the giant forest hog that had terrified me so much when I was young appeared to me there. They came right up to me as though I was just part of the herd.

If I reached out to touch them, would my hand pass through their bodies as if I were a ghost? I was afraid to try. They never stayed with me for long, disappearing again into the forest, and before I knew it, I would be back inside the hut.

But though everyone seemed to have expected it, I didn't die. Gradually, I began to regain consciousness, and against all odds I began to recover.

Once I could think straight again, I started to wonder if my illness was a sign from Allah telling me it was time for me to reconsider what I was doing with my life. Was I meant to use my degree and increased knowledge to succeed in the city, to make money for my family and myself? Or was I meant to come back here?

My mother and father made no secret about wanting me to return home to live with them. Maybe to teach in the new village school building. To coach soccer and work with some of my young students on the farm. Sooner or later to take a wife—or wives, which was permissible in our culture—and raise grandchildren to continue our tribal and family name.

My Uncle Sekou saw in my illness and miraculous survival an even greater significance. He'd been suggesting to my father for some time that I return home to begin training more deeply in Islam and become his apprentice with an eye toward my eventually succeeding him as local imam. Uncle Sekou had five wives (technically under Islam, he was permitted only four wives, but no one seemed to mind) and seemed to have a good life. Maybe my parents were right. Maybe my entire life had been leading up to this moment in time and this sickness was a result of Allah's plan for my life—to teach me once and for all to submit to the way of his prophet Muhammad and to my parents' authority, and to live and blossom here at home with my family.

A few days into my convalescence, I was able to sit up and take nourishment for the first time in more than two weeks. Mama hovered over me, feeding me a bowl of broth. "You're feeling better, Kono."

I nodded, thankful for her comforting presence.

"That's good." She fed me another spoonful.

Over time, my strength returned, and I was finally able to get out of bed and move around. Everyone seemed baffled, including our local witch doctor, who'd apparently also been expecting me to die, although he was pleased to take whatever credit he could for my recovery.

I wanted to honor my parents, and my village's customs and traditions, so I went along with whatever conclusions they wanted to make about my illness. But somewhere deep in my soul, I began to sense it wasn't the witch doctor's magic nor all the prayers and talismans that had made me well. Something bigger was at work. Something was going to happen in my life. I just didn't know what it was yet. The first few bricks of the walls of fear I'd built up over the course of my life were beginning to be torn down, by what God or power I could not yet begin to imagine.

***

Since I was the first person from my village to finish high school, it did seem Allah's will that I would find myself still in Balumah a few weeks later, in a ramshackle single-room schoolhouse organizing the day's lesson plan surrounded by young students. Teaching school and coaching soccer in my village weren't at all what I'd envisioned for myself when I'd left for Monrovia years before, but I decided to make the best of the situation. After all, any of these children could easily have been me a dozen years before.

The school in our village served a hundred and fifty students ranging in age from five to sixteen. Most would never complete their education. They would come to class sporadically for a few grades, maybe learn a few things, then drop out to marry and have children of their own or to work in the fields or at some other sort of physical labor. What was I to make of their potential? I could see hope and fear in their eyes, curiosity coupled with hesitancy, eagerness coupled with resignation.

Everyone was hoping things would remain peaceful and continue to improve for those of us in the interior, although from what I'd begun to hear, the latest signs from Monrovia weren't good. Doe was still promising free elections, but he and his People's Redemption Council—made up of mostly members of the Does' Krahn tribe—seemed to be mainly jockeying for positions of power and fighting over the spoils of what they'd attained. This included purging from any position of power members of other tribes and anyone else who opposed them, making them little different despite their rhetoric than the Tolbert regime they'd brutally displaced.

I'd never taught school before, but I'd watched enough teachers operate over the years to be able to mimic their strategies to some degree. There were two other teachers, both of them women, neither of whom had gone as far as I had in school. Being the only male teacher posed its challenges, but since I was originally from the village, many families and children saw in me someone they could emulate who had gone away, received an education, and had now returned to share what he'd learned with them.

We didn't have many textbooks, but the few we did have served as an adequate springboard for learning. Most of the students still couldn't read or write. This made working with any kind of book a challenge. So I learned to improvise, using whatever props I could scratch up, such as vegetables and stones to teach math or charcoal and bark for writing and reading.

I received no salary for teaching in the school. The village had no money for that. Instead, the community compensated my family through collective labor and food they brought to us. The labor was important. Teachers were honored in our tribe and village, not because people valued education so much, but because to pay for primary school—which virtually no students could afford—a teacher's pupils were obligated to work on the teacher's family's farm.

My renewed presence and the extra workers for our family farm seemed to gladden the heart of my father. For once, my books and learning were proving useful to him. He not only welcomed the help in the fields, but I imagine he saw in my keener interest in Islam a reflection of his own heart. Maybe, like him, I was striving to overcome my fear and shame by living in denial. Fear, on the surface at least, could at least be kept walled off through pride, religious discipline, and when necessary, anger.

One afternoon after classes had ended and the students had left to pursue their labors, I stepped outside to look out over the jungle settlement that had been my entire world in early years. The sun had begun to angle beneath the treetops as it broke through clouds of rain, making a rainbow above the thatched roofs of the village. A cacophony of birds, insects, and monkeys came from the surrounding rainforest.

It wasn't at all like Monrovia, but maybe there could be a livable life for me here, a life of relative plenty carved out of impoverishment—with multiple wives if I wanted—and a prosperous farm and a life embraced by my village, my parents' tribes, and my extended family. I could follow in the footsteps of my ancestors, shove fear and shame to the side, and keep them locked away in separate chambers of my mind.

I closed the door of the school behind me with a sense of pride and headed out into the warm mist.

***

Sometime during that year, I remember following my Uncle Sekou as he walked along the edge of a field of elephant grass teaching me *surah*—verses from the Quran.

> In the name of Allah, Most Gracious, Most Merciful.
> Praise be to Allah, the Cherisher and Sustainer of the worlds;
> Most Gracious, Most Merciful;
> Master of the Day of Judgment.
> Thee do we worship, and Thine aid we seek.
> Show us the straight way,
> The way of those on whom Thou hast bestowed Thy Grace,
> Those whose (portion) is not wrath, and who go not astray.

A stocky man with an erudite manner and a neatly trimmed goatee, Uncle Sekou moved with a cautious grace over the mounds of dirt and overturned soil. My students and I had already been out to "brush" the farm—preparing the soil to plant this year's crop. I respected Uncle Sekou and appreciated the time he spent with me. Since recovering from my illness, I'd started regularly attending the mosque, no longer just out of duty or obligation, but out of a serious desire to learn.

> I seek refuge in the Lord of mankind, the King of mankind, the God of mankind, From the evil of the sneaking whisper, who whispers in the hearts of mankind, of the jinn and of mankind.

Once the school year was over, I spent even more time with Uncle Sekou. He explained to me the Islamic belief in *jinn*, or mystical, sometimes demonic spirits. As our village imam, Uncle Sekou possessed a special cultural and political power among our tribe. Many viewed him as a soothsayer who possessed special power on a par with the local witch doctor. Our version of folk Islam fit right in with our traditional belief in ancestral and bush spirits. These spirits, along with secret societies, had the most impact on daily life. Secrecy was paramount.

The mystical side of Islam appealed to me. Even Muhammad had feared demonic spirits. Uncle Sekou saw no inconsistency in going to the mosque and praying toward Mecca five times a day, then spending time with the witch doctor for protection from evil spirits. Or reciting a Muslim chant believed to be a powerful deterrent against jinn—*Rokia, roukia, rukia, roqya, ruqya*—as a defense against black magic. When he looked at me, Uncle Sekou must have seen a young, bright, and well-educated pupil who'd become his heir apparent as the next village imam to carry on the message of Islam.

Was I already beginning to think like Uncle Sekou, like an

imam, drawing upon the deepest reservoirs of our faith, then passing them on to others? Sometimes I would lay awake at night, feeling the spiritual warfare for my soul. An oppressive fear hovered over my self-discipline.

Submit, submit, submit.

This was our Islam.

***

Partway through that summer, my cousin Joseph arrived in Balumah to enjoy a holiday break before heading back to Monrovia for his second year at the University of Liberia. I could see he felt good about where he was heading in life, and I was happy for him. Joseph was not just my cousin but a good friend. I especially appreciated that he viewed me as someone capable of doing big things and making a difference in Liberia and the world.

Joseph hadn't embraced religion the way I did. He dabbled in Christianity and other faiths when it suited him, but he didn't take any of them too seriously. Like most Liberians, he could invoke the name of God and put on a show of religiosity when it suited him. One night we stayed up late talking, and I could tell he was trying to figure out how surviving my illness had changed me.

Shortly before his return to Monrovia, he made me an offer. "Why don't you come with me back to the city, Tony? Just for a few days, maybe a week. Either Kumar will give you a place to stay or I will. It will cost you nothing."

Go back to Monrovia? Where I'd been given up for dead?

At first, I wasn't too keen about the idea. Then I thought, why not? I'd established myself well enough in the village. The next school term wasn't scheduled to begin for a few weeks, and it would be good to see Kumar, my big sister and her husband again, and maybe make a few connections with old high school classmates and friends like Joseph. The more I thought about it, the more I began to like Joseph's idea. It would be good for me and maybe even strengthen my faith in Allah to take a break from Balumah and spend some time back in the city.

***

Packing up a few things, I said my goodbyes to my parents and the rest of the family. The next morning, Joseph and I were up before sunrise. We were in no hurry as we set out walking toward Monrovia. I was skilled in the ways of the jungle, and Joseph was a good traveling companion. We hiked along trails through the forest for a full day and made camp that night.

After nearly two days of talking and laughing together, we finally reached a road where Joseph had arranged for a friend with a vehicle to pick us up. The friend eventually arrived in a van that had clearly seen better days. The engine ran well enough, but the seats were cracked and ripped in many places while the floorboards had large holes through which you could look down and see the ground.

Still, the driver's beaming grin indicated confidence in his vehicle. Joseph introduced us. Then we threw our bags in the back and climbed in. A tall, thin man, Joseph's friend proved a jovial sort whose smile seemed permanently affixed to his face. He had a skin condition that had caused a loss of pigmentation in spots, making his bare arms and face a patchwork of dark and light.

The road was unpaved, rocky, and rutted, slamming our heads against the ceiling unless we grabbed the edge of the seat. As we bounced toward Monrovia, the driver turned on the van's radio. It was tuned to a popular Christian station, ELWA. I'd listened to the station before while living in Monrovia, especially the news programming, but I'd paid little attention to the preaching or Christian music.

Today though, I was a captive audience, so I began listening. After a couple of songs, the program shifted to some sort of radio drama. The show was called *Unshackled*, and I'd never heard anything like it before.

Apparently uninterested, Joseph, who was sitting up front beside the driver, began talking with his friend right over the voice of the narrator. But they didn't turn the radio down, and I could hear the program clearly through the van's rear speakers. I listened quietly, captivated by the drama's storyline. I don't remember the details of that particular episode, but some of the narrator's words seemed to attach themselves to my heart and soul: "This whole program is about how to face yourself and think."

Face yourself and think. What did the man mean? How was I supposed to face myself? I'd been taught that all I needed to do was submit to Allah and follow the way of the prophet. The prophet and our traditions taught that it was unholy and potentially dangerous to focus on oneself at all, that I shouldn't even look at myself naked in a mirror. As for thinking, what was I supposed to think about? What did this radio narrator mean when he told me to *face myself*?

My perception of Christianity had developed from my friends and classmates who claimed to be Christian and how they lived. None had ever spoken directly with me about Jesus or faith. I saw them going to church, but I'd always figured it was for social and power-seeking reasons. They seemed to treat Jesus and the Christian church like their own personal talismans. To me, Christians displayed the worst kind of weakness—a lack of spiritual and emotional discipline that led only to chaos and debaucheries.

But all the way to Monrovia, I continued to reflect on what I'd heard the man on the radio say. I had to admit that for some time I'd recognized there was something missing in me. No matter how much I submitted to Allah and disciplined my actions and behavior, I couldn't find a sustainable solution for my fear. I was thirsty to the depths of my soul for a peace and freedom I knew must exist somewhere. But the more I enmeshed myself in the self-disciplines and recitations of Islam, and the more I dabbled in African animism, magic, and witchcraft, the thirstier I became.

It felt like I was drinking dust.

***

We arrived back in Monrovia in the summer of 1983, a few weeks before my twenty-second birthday. Joseph had promised to honor my desire to return to Balumah to teach, but after only a few days he began pressuring me to stay.

"I knew I wouldn't win arguing with you back in the village, Tony. But now that you're here, I want you to listen to what I have to say. You are no longer a country villager at heart. You're a city man, and you deserve more. You deserve to go to college in this new Liberia and work your way into what we are building here under President Doe."

In his mind, Joseph had things all mapped out for me,

starting with joining him as a student at the University of
Liberia, where I'd already passed the entrance exam and
had planned to attend prior to my illness. I wasn't so easily
convinced.

"My father thinks I've matured since my sickness. He
believes I have a future in Balumah as a school teacher and
coaching soccer. If I stay here instead of going back, Papa will
be very upset. So will Uncle Sekou. He has already started
training me to succeed him as village imam."

Joseph was silent for a moment. Then he said: "I'm sure
that must be a great honor, Tony. No offense, but if you're
really meant to be an imam, then you need to come here to go
to college. The traditions and teachings of people like Uncle
Sekou can only take you so far. You and I both know you're
not a soldier like your father or my father. You're meant to do
something different."

"What about you?" I asked.

"My plan is clear. I plan to finish college and join the Army
like my father."

"You'll be an officer then."

"Yes." He poked me in the chest and laughed. "And right
now, I'm ordering my favorite country cousin to stay here in
the city and finish what you started. High school was only the
beginning for you."

When the time came for me to return to the village, I wrote
to my parents to tell them I planned to remain in Monrovia
a while longer. I was still planning to return home eventually,
but the longer I stayed in the city the more I became convinced
my cousin Joseph was right. I needed to forge a different path
for myself.

I finally wrote another letter to my parents to say I would

not be returning to Balumah. I'd saved up a bit of money, so I decided to make the necessary arrangements for attending the University of Liberia that fall. Once again, I had no idea that God had an entirely different path in mind for me.

***

Not long after I mailed the letter to my parents, I received an invitation to attend a small gathering at a house in Monrovia. It was an evening in the middle of the week, and I was told there would be a Bible study going on. I found nothing unusual or alarming about such a gathering. The majority of Liberians were Christian, and many spent time each week in church and praying to their god. I'd also heard about these kinds of house meetings where people studied the Christian holy book. I was actually looking forward to this opportunity to explain to these Christians that Jesus was neither God nor the son of God, but a prophet sent by Allah to proclaim the *injil*, or gospel, of the future coming of the Prophet Muhammad.

Rain fell on my way to the house gathering. Arriving at the address, water draining from the roof sounded a steady drumbeat against the fabric of my umbrella as I knocked on the door. A young woman answered my knock. I introduced myself. "My name is Tony Weedor. I'm not sure if I have the right address. I was invited to a study meeting."

"Of course. Please come in. You're very welcome here." The young woman looked harmless enough, and without hesitation I followed her into a small foyer and parlor, on the far side of which I could see a larger room where a sizable group of men and women about my age was gathered; some seated on folding chairs, others cross-legged on the floor. Most appeared to be native Liberians like me. They were singing Christian hymns, and it suddenly dawned on me that this might be more than just a Bible study. There was clearly Christian worship going on as well.

I wasn't quite sure how to react to the situation, since I was wary of being drawn into any non-Muslim worship or prayer. By the time I found a seat against the back wall, however, the music had thankfully come to a stop. Then someone stepped out into the middle of the semicircle and began speaking. I was shocked to see that this person everyone had come to hear was a middle-aged white woman. She spoke in English, and her accent sounded American like so many of the expatriates who lived and worked in Monrovia.

She introduced herself as Pauline Sonius, and said she was from Iowa, in the United States. I didn't know anything about Iowa, but this woman seemed different than other Americans I'd met.

Physically, she didn't seem imposing, standing only about five feet tall. Her clothing was typical Western slacks and blouse, and her hair was modestly wrapped in a dark blue West African *kente* cloth scarf. I felt instantly drawn to what she was saying, however, as much by her serene demeanor as her message; her light features and blue eyes radiated a kindness and understanding I'd never seen before.

Miss Pauline spoke of a love beyond all understanding and about Jesus being God and dying on a cross as a sacrifice for all of our sins, then returning from the dead to live again. I knew this story from reading Muslim apologetics about the Bible. Muslims believed in Jesus, too, of course. The Quran honored him as a great prophet just below Muhammad, the greatest of all prophets. But the idea that Jesus had died on a cross or that he was somehow God was nothing but a Christian lie. How could Allah have been dead for three days?

Still, the way this woman spoke about Jesus made a deep impression on me. I'd never heard anyone speak about him in such a personal, loving way, almost as though he was her closest friend. She continued talking about the power of Jesus to forgive sins and how grace supersedes all when it comes to God. At one point, her gaze rested on me, taking in my traditional Muslim garb of long-sleeved white shirt and *Kufi* skullcap; but I saw in her eyes no challenge to or fear of my presence—rather, a warm love and acceptance. This woman seemed to genuinely care for everyone in the room and for me, just the way I was. I looked around the room. The other young people all seemed to be listening intently; a few even offered me welcoming nods and smiles as well.

The American talked a bit more about something she called "being born again." Then she mentioned looking at oneself in the mirror. This immediately caught my attention, and my thoughts flashed back to the radio program I'd heard in the car driving into Monrovia on the topic of "facing yourself."

I was still thinking about those words when everyone else suddenly rose to their feet and began to sing again, "In the name of Jesus we have the victory."

Victory over what? I wondered. Wasn't Jesus executed by the Romans on a cross? That was hardly victorious!

The answer came several stanzas into the song. It was victory over death itself. They went on singing, "In the name of Jesus, demons will have to flee."

Demons flee? I could hardly believe my ears. Demons were something to be respected and feared, something to be warded off by rote prayers, charms, talismans, animal sacrifices, and interventions from the imam or witch doctor. Demons weren't something to be trifled with by simply throwing out the name of Jesus.

The song finally ended. Then the missionary continued speaking, this time about Jesus being alive and his Holy Spirit being present within us. But I couldn't get the song lyrics out of my head. I had no intention of being rude or confrontational, but I was so distraught that I jumped up and interrupted the woman.

"What do you mean 'demons flee?' In the song you just sang, you said 'In the name of Jesus, demons will flee?' How could this man Jesus have power over such things?"

She seemed neither insulted nor disturbed by my question. She patiently explained again that Jesus was divine, the son of God. As such, he had absolute power over supernatural beings and presences that might try to overcome us with fear. At his command and in his name, demons were forced to flee.

I didn't believe any of this, of course, but for one moment, I could feel the presence of God's Holy Spirit, a visceral presence tugging at my heart. This was accompanied by an overwhelming sense of peace, a love for me that was so pure and intense and holy I could barely stand. For the first time in my life, my fears seemed to melt away. It was as if they'd never existed.

Something was stirring in my soul that went beyond man's religion, mosques, and churches. I had to exercise every bit of self-control I could muster to keep from completely dissolving into tears. Was it possible this Jesus of Nazareth really did possess some kind of a power I'd never understood? Could there really be a direct, personal relationship with a holy God?

After the song, the American opened the Bible in her hands and turned to Philippians 4:7:

And the peace of God, which transcends all understanding, will guard your hearts and your minds in Christ Jesus.

Peace? In Monrovia, I saw little peace even under native Liberian rule, only fear, turmoil, infighting, increasing tribalism, and a still smoldering anger. Even in Islam, I realized, I was starving for peace. Muhammad had shown us how to live in complete submission to Allah, what to pray, and what to do. But he had not shown us how to think for ourselves or how to find that of which this woman had spoken—freedom from fear.

I also realized that the peace this woman spoke of was a peace that had no political context. It was a personal peace that transcended the external, a peace, as the words she'd read indicated, that no human mind could understand.

I stood fixed to the spot as the young people around me started singing again. I didn't know what it all meant, but I desperately wanted the kind of peace the missionary had described.

Not lacking for boldness, when the singing stopped and the missionary started speaking again, I raised my hand and interrupted her once more; I asked her what I needed to do to follow Jesus. The room grew silent as all eyes turned to Pauline Sonius and me. She didn't hesitate.

"I will tell you," she said. *"If you declare with your mouth, 'Jesus is Lord,' and believe in your heart that God raised him from the dead, you will be saved,"* she quoted from Romans 10:9.

I realized I was broken. I knew she was telling the truth. I told her I was ready to do exactly as she'd described. Me, a broken, fearful young Muslim with a confident, religious exterior I'd discovered in my heart wasn't real.

There, in front of the whole room of people, the missionary led me in the "sinner's prayer."

"Heavenly Father, I know that I am a sinner and that I deserve to go to hell. I believe that Jesus Christ died on the cross for my sins. I do now receive him as my Lord and personal Savior. I promise to serve you to the best of my ability. Please save me. In Jesus' name, Amen."

Decades later, I've remained in contact with some of the people who were at the Bible study in Monrovia that day. They still tell me they've never seen a conversion quite so publicly dramatic. I wish I could say a lightning bolt physically struck the room in that moment, but it didn't. Instead, I felt a spiritual bolt of lightning in my heart, soul, and mind.

***

That night, I slept more soundly than I had in months. When I woke up the next morning, I felt like a new man. Something deep and spiritual had shifted in my life. It was like flipping on an electrical switch, stepping out of the darkness into the light.

The following day, I purchased a Bible. Though I'd read parts of it before, I now began studying it with new eyes. I read through chapter four of the Apostle Paul's letter to the Philippians in the Christian New Testament several times and sat meditating on some of the words:

Rejoice in the Lord always. I will say it again: Rejoice! Let your gentleness be evident to all. The Lord is near. Do not be anxious about anything, but in every situation, by prayer and petition, with thanksgiving, present your requests to God. And the peace of God, which transcends all understanding, will guard your hearts and your minds in Christ Jesus. Finally, brothers and sisters, whatever is true, whatever is noble, whatever is right, whatever is pure, whatever is lovely, whatever is admirable—if anything is excellent or praiseworthy— think about such things. Whatever you have learned or received or heard from me or seen in me, put it into practice. And the God of peace will be with you. (Philippians 4:4-9)

Over the next few weeks, I met with a number of others who'd attended the meeting that night. I also heard Miss Pauline, who I came to learn was a Christian missionary, speak again and found out that she led a weekly Bible study. I attended a few more of these meetings, at times finding myself confused, but overall feeling so much joy I could hardly contain myself. As impossible as it may have seemed, nothing would ever be the same for me. I'd accepted Jesus into my heart, and the peace I felt was so incredible I had to know more.

I started attending church. Soon thereafter, Pastor Bill Ross of the Monrovia Evangelical Church baptized me in the ocean at a special ceremony on the beach. The morning after I was baptized, I went to my closet and put on blue jeans and a simple T-shirt. Then I boxed up my Muslim clothing, Quran, and other Muslim writings. I left the container filled with these things on the steps of Monrovia's central mosque and walked away.

Continuing on to the river, I threw all of my charm necklaces, prayer beads, amulets, and other folk Islamic implements into the water. The amulet and prayer beads floated for a while along the surface of the water before beginning to sink. I watched them be caught by the current downstream until at last the muddy water swallowed them.

I still had much to learn about what following Jesus meant, but I knew my life, from then on, would never be the same. Whatever power those physical objects had held over me, along with the shame and the fear I'd known my whole life, was gone.

CHAPTER TWELVE

Chapel

In the spring of 2004, I was asked to speak during morning chapel ceremonies at my alma mater, Denver Theological Seminary. The organizers wanted me to talk about my experiences as a former Muslim and now, as a professor of Islamic history. Outside the chapel building, while the air still held onto its winter chill, tulips and irises planted in the fall had begun to bloom.

I took some time preparing my remarks.

The upcoming American presidential election dominated the headlines at that time; President George W. Bush faced ongoing criticism about his decision to invade Iraq in the midst of a difficult re-election campaign. That spring, he began intensifying his efforts to woo American voters and convince them to stay the course when it came to his foreign policy, fighting terrorism, and furthering his domestic social agenda.

Through SIM International, my family and I had been granted R-1 Temporary Religious Worker visas to remain in America. I'd also hired an immigration attorney to begin the long application process to become an American citizen. My attorney warned me to be careful with my public statements about Islam. Ever since the historic attacks of 9/11, President Bush and his spokespeople had remained very cautious—some might even say circumspect—when making statements about Islam. The official position was that Islam was "a religion of peace" while the 9/11 attackers and other Islamic terrorists were portrayed as extremists outside the mainstream teachings of Islam.

As my attorney explained, US State Department officials reviewing my citizenship application might not look kindly on any criticism I might level at the Bush administration—for example, that much of early Islamic history contradicted Bush's public statements. As a teacher of Islamic history, I understood this to be true. Muhammad's constant violent attacks against non-Muslim territories were perhaps the most glaring examples; in particular, his public beheading of over six hundred Jews in Qurayza who, after failing to resist his militarism, had attempted to form an alliance against him.

At the same time, I understood that many millions of Muslims practiced a religion that through various deviations from orthodox Islam attempted to ignore and move beyond, at least on a personal level, these uncomfortable truths. I taught Christian missionaries that it was important to understand the difference between Muslims and Islam. To an evangelical Christian, Islam as a religion was indefensible. But as people, Muslims were no different than us. They were human beings and sinners just as we were and equally deserving of God's forgiveness and love.

As a former Muslim with many family members who remained Muslim at the time, my teaching wasn't based on theory or supposition but direct experience. I was interested in building relationships—in the truth about fear, religion, and the human condition. As a Christian, I'd begun to understand that God never stops seeking the hearts of the lost, that He was calling me to be a witness to His great love, and that on some level, we all yearn for true peace and freedom in our hearts.

While refusing to turn a blind eye to the facts about orthodox Islam and terrorism, I did my best to communicate my beliefs about God's love to those at the chapel ceremony in Colorado that day. I was glad I wasn't the president or another politician. I didn't feel the need to look the other way or twist myself inside out when it came to spiritual reality in order to juggle a need for secular popularity and the geopolitical necessity of working alongside Muslim allies in the war on terror.

I didn't think God had been surprised by the 9/11 attacks or anything else. More than two thousand years after Jesus, the Messiah, died and was resurrected from the dead, He still loves all of us through the power of his Holy Spirit. He comes after us anyway—even when we all, like fearful lost sheep, have gone astray.

CHAPTER THIRTEEN

Run!

The day my mother disowned me, she appeared in the door-way of the house where I was staying in Monrovia, resplen-dent in her *al-amira* veil. This shawl head covering, the soft one she reserved for trading in the city, wrapped around her shoulders and hid her hair but left her face visible.

It had been several months since I'd heard the missionary from Iowa speak and thrown out my voodoo implements, Islamic amulets, and charms. Since then, I'd attended quite a number of Bible studies and was growing more and more comfortable with my newfound faith.

The afternoon was warm as usual, and a ceiling fan ticked slowly overhead. In the streets outside, a few cars passed backed and forth, but overall traffic had dwindled signifi-cantly since the coup and takeover by Doe's military regime.

"Mama!" I bowed as she entered.

She greeted me in the traditional Muslim style, which was, in fact, Arabic instead of any of the languages we actually spoke in Liberia. *"As-Salaam-Alaikum."*

I returned the greeting. "And upon you peace."

Mama seemed tired and suspicious. She looked over my Western-style clothing. Perhaps she'd already heard about my conversion. In those days, communication to the interior by telephone or mail was often difficult, but tribal messages passed from person to person could spread quickly, although much might be lost in translation.

For many in Monrovia, fear of the current government was beginning to replace past resentments over the oppression and exploitations of the Americo-Liberians. So maybe Mama had simply grown concerned about the reasons for my prolonged absence and my failure to return to our village as promised.

As I hugged her, Mama's familiar pleasant smell—a blend of the tobacco, nutmeg, and ginger she sold in the market-place—filled my nostrils.

"Why didn't you tell me you were coming?"

"I'm sorry if I startled you, Kono. I wanted to surprise you."

It had been a long time since she'd called me Kono—my nickname given to me at birth.

"I'm so glad you're here," I said. "There is so much I want to talk to you about."

"Wonderful," she said. "I want to hear it all."

Maybe she hadn't, after all, heard about my decision to follow Jesus. Or if she had, maybe she didn't want to believe it.

"I've missed you," I said.

"I've missed you, too. Are you okay?"

"Better than you might imagine."

"Praise be to Allah. I've been worried about you."

"How is Papa doing?"

"Your father is in decent health, but his work is hard. The rice harvest hasn't been good this season. He just returned from the city where he went to pick up his military pension."

"Papa was here? In Monrovia?"

"Yes."

"Why didn't he come to see me?"

"Perhaps it was not safe for him."

From the glint in her eyes, I understood she was lying. Mama also understood that I knew she was being untruthful. We Liberians have a word for this kind of understanding of one another, an oft-used interjection: *Kukujumuku.* It literally means "You not inside; you not know."

Mama didn't use this word when it came to my father, but she might as well have.

No doubt he was still angry with me because of my decision to leave home—and doubly angry at my failure to return home. If he'd been in Monrovia, he'd no doubt spoken to my uncle and quite probably heard of my decision to follow Jesus. That must have felt like a knife to the throat for him.

"Are you sure you are safe here, Tony?" Mama asked, still dancing around the issue of why she'd really come.

"Yes. I'm safe."

"Many have disappeared from our area, you know. Even more, I hear, from Monrovia."

"I know."

There was a long pause as Mama looked around the room. "Much has changed here in the city, hasn't it?"

I wasn't sure where she was going with the question. "Mama, why have you come here today?"

She stepped to the window and looked out at the street but said nothing.

I repeated my question.

Mama set her bag on the floor. "I made the journey to buy

some things in the market, and I wanted to see what you were up to, Abdullah. I've heard rumors."

Rumors? I wondered what she might have heard and why she was using my Islamic name. Names are important in Liberia. Before the Doe government, my name, Tony Weedor, was considered a source of shame because it indicated I was lowborn and not among the ruling Americo-Liberian families. That was no longer the case. One of my distant uncles was even said to be helping run one of Doe's prisons.

Still, I realized none of these things were what had brought my mother to see me. "Can I get you something to eat or drink?"

"No, thank you," she said. "I bought something on the street."

We sat down together on the floor cushions that were common living room furnishings in Liberia. For the next several minutes, we talked about home. We talked about my brother Austin, the oldest, and his continued troubles. Mama also gave me updates about Alfred, my next oldest brother, and my sisters Victoria and Zinnah.

Our conversation brought back memories of growing up with all of them, especially walking with my brothers to work on our farm, splashing through a muddy stream on the way with the rising heat of the sun on our backs. My thoughts flashed back to my Grandma Zinnah's simple act of love in pouring water on my head in front of the hating crowd after I'd burned down the rice kitchen as a young child.

That memory carried a new and powerful meaning for me now that I'd accepted Jesus into my life. The shed blood of Jesus had washed away my sins and left me spiritually clean and forgiven just as my grandmother's deluge of water had symbolically swept away my guilt.

Finally, Mama came to the real purpose of her visit. "Abdullah, servant of Allah, your Uncle Sekou has been asking after you."

"Oh? What does the imam ask of me?"

"He wonders if you might reconsider your decision to leave. He wonders if you might return to our village to continue your training to take his place as our next imam."

"Is this Uncle Sekou asking or are you and Papa asking?"

"Both," she said.

I hesitated. Her gaze seemed to bore into me. In the past, I might have wilted under such a look, but now I felt different. A feeling of calm settled over me, one I'd never felt before.

Mama's usual composure shifted ever so slightly as if something she knew to be true but feared and didn't want to be true had entered her mind. It was as if she was doing her best to push the thought away.

"I have something important to tell you," I said.

"Yes? What is it?"

"You know that as part of my training in Islam I have been reading the Christian Bible."

"Yes. I imagine you have."

"Not too long ago, I grew more curious about Jesus in the course of my studies, and began seeking out more information. I read more and more, and I also attended a Christian meeting to learn better how to defend Islam."

"You have always been a scholar. That's why your uncle sees so much potential in you."

"I know, but things have changed."

"Really? What things have changed?"

"My heart has changed. About Jesus."

"You mean Jesus of Nazareth in the Christian Bible."

"Yes."

"What are you saying, Kono?"

"I've become a Christian, Mama."

The air seemed to escape from the room. My mother stared at me, blinking, as though I'd switched to a different language she couldn't comprehend, or didn't want to comprehend. Then her eyes brimmed with tears. She wiped them away with the back of her hand as she pushed off her cushion and rose to her feet. "I don't understand."

I stood along with her. "I've put my faith in Jesus Christ of Nazareth. I believe he is the Son of the one true God."

"Blasphemy. You know there is no God but Allah and Muhammad is his messenger."

I shook my head. "No, I believe what the Christians teach is true. God is a holy trinity—Father, Son, and Holy Spirit—and Jesus offers us all forgiveness, hope, and salvation through his death on a cross and his resurrection from the dead."

"Nonsense." Mama took a step back, placing her hand over her chest as if she'd been struck. "Resurrection from the dead? Son of God. Father, Son, and Holy Spirit? What sorcery is this?"

"I've learned it's all true," I said. "And it leads to a peace and a freedom like nothing I could have ever imagined."

Like a lot of new Christians, I suppose, I was giving her both barrels of preaching all at once because I couldn't help it. The words came tumbling out of my mouth. Mama took a step backward as if to try to gain some distance from what I was saying.

"How can you be seduced by such ridiculous ideas? You, of all people, Tony. I fear you have lost your mind."

In that moment, I remembered something. In my pocket was another folk Islamic implement I'd found earlier that morning in a drawer. It was a charm bracelet my mother and father had given me in my childhood when I'd shared my fears about another village boy being bitten by a snake. The bracelet was supposed to protect me from such bites.

Reaching into my pocket, I pulled out the bracelet and handed it to my mother. "Here, Mama, I no longer need this because I'm not afraid anymore. Jesus is always with me. I wish I could help you understand how much peace He has brought to my life."

"The son of Mary?" She quoted the reference from the Quran. "You speak of him as if he is alive."

"He is, Mama, just as the Bible promises. He was raised from the dead on the third day just as the Hebrew prophets foretold. He is God, one with the Father, Yahweh. And his Holy Spirit is alive in me."

Now I'd gone too far. Mama began to sob and shake her head. "Can you even begin to realize what this will do to our family? Do you have any idea the shame this will bring upon all of us?"

"I'm sorry, Mama, I—"

"No, you're not. How can you proclaim such things? After all we've done for you. You've been bewitched by some of your Americo teachers or some of these Christians you have met."

"That's not it at all," I said.

Mama's trembling fingers clutched the bracelet as she sobbed and wailed softly for a few minutes more, my strong Mandingo mother reduced to grief beyond her control. I felt terrible. I put out a hand to comfort her, but she pushed it away.

Then her back stiffened, and her expression went blank. With the end of her veil, she dried her tears. Bending down, she picked up the bag with her purchases from the market and turned to leave.

"Please don't go," I said, reaching out a hand.

"Don't touch me!" She looked back at me with a pain and coldness in her eyes I'd never seen before. "I was afraid it would come down to this."

"So you knew? You already knew I'd become a Christian?"

"Of course I knew. We'd already heard rumors about your bewitchment, but I had to come see for myself if they were true."

"But, Mama, listen—"

She held up her hand, commanding me to stop. "I have only one thing to tell you. And this is from your father and the rest of our family, too. Run!"

"What?"

"You heard me, Tony. Run!"

CHAPTER FOURTEEN

People Magazine

In the spring of 2004, an issue of *People Magazine* ended up on the coffee table of our apartment in Denver. The front cover showed a striking photo of actor Charlie Sheen posing with his then-wife actress Denise Richards along with their newborn baby. They looked every bit the happy couple. I supposed that was the photographer's intent, since the headline read HELLO BABY! HE CHANGES THE BABY AND THE BABY CHANGES HIM.

The staging of the photo and the headline made me smile, not because I knew much about Charlie Sheen or Denise Richards. But seeing them together reminded me of my marriage to Beth and of our four children, and of how we'd almost lost one another along the way and how it had all begun in a troubled Liberia nearly two decades before. It was a time and a place that seemed very far removed from this glossy American magazine cover.

CHAPTER FIFTEEN

Who Is That Girl?

I have no doubt my father boiled with rage after learning about my conversion to Christianity. I wrote a letter to him and Mama, trying my best to lovingly explain my new faith. *How could they not know? How could they not see?* I wondered. I hoped they might at least be curious about my decision to follow Jesus, but they never responded.

Worse, they effectively disowned me, as did most of the rest of my family. They let it be known that I was not to be further encouraged or supported in any way by the family. I suppose I had now become as good as dead to them, especially to my father and uncle and one aunt who was particularly devout in her Muslim faith. The religious shame my conversion brought to the family was deep, and maybe the pain was just too difficult for them to bear. I imagine the pain was even more acute for Mama and Grandma Zinnah, who'd not only nurtured me and taught me lessons about being Muslim from an early age but had shielded me from my father's tantrums. Still, their failure to respond to my letters and others that followed stung my heart.

From then on, I had little or no contact with anyone from Balumah. I felt both sad and guilty at times. I came to understand all too well that to step outside one's familial support in Africa was tantamount to an emotional death sentence. Every time depression threatened to overwhelm me, I would delve deeper into the Bible, taking comfort in God's presence and the stories of believers before me who'd suffered. One verse in particular brought me great comfort.

And the God of all grace, who called you to his eternal glory in Christ, after you have suffered a little while, will himself restore you and make you strong, firm, and steadfast. (1 Peter 5:10)

Though I no longer lived with Kumar, the Indian businessman remained a friend. I took to hanging around the ELWA radio station, which was run by SIM International, the missionary organization for which Pauline Sonius worked. I was visiting her office at ELWA one day when a young expatriate who looked North American or European walked in. Pauline introduced him as a SIM missionary from Germany.

Then Pauline said something to him I didn't expect.

"Hardy, this young believer is driving me crazy around here. Tony needs a job."

Thus began my lifelong friendship with Hartmut Stricker. Hartmut, whom all his friends referred to as "Hardy," worked as a missionary in and around Bomi Hills, the same town where I'd gone to school many years before. Hardy took a few moments to look me over, then said simply, "Come with me."

He led me outside onto a verandah and for the next couple

of hours seemed to be conducting an employment interview. He asked about my background. He quizzed me at length about the Bible, asking a number of questions about my faith. He seemed to be testing my authenticity as a follower of Jesus. I can't remember what I told him exactly, but I must have gotten a few things right.

Hardy then explained that he'd been praying for God to send him a local believer familiar with the Bomi Hills area who spoke the different tribal languages and could help him spread the word about Jesus. He wondered out loud if I might be God's answer to his prayer. In exchange for my working with him as a traveling evangelist, he said, he could provide me a place to stay and buy me a scooter to travel around the area.

I jumped at the opportunity.

For the next several months, I lived and worked closely with Hardy, growing steadily in my knowledge of the Bible. I soon became a fixture on the roads as we traveled all around Bomi Hills and back and forth to Monrovia. I also got to know many people from the churches in the area. To my disappointment, I discovered that for many Liberians faith in Jesus was just a superficial lip service, a cultural remnant no different from folk Islam that had been handed down to them by their parents, not something they'd taken to heart or applied to their everyday lives. I tried to serve as a witness to these people as well.

More than anything else, Hardy helped feed my hunger for God's Word. He helped cultivate within me a desire to read the Scriptures I carry with me to this day. My time spent reading the Bible was so long, in fact, that I literally wore out several printed copies. Hardy would laugh with delight each time I had to come to him asking for a new Bible.

A thirst for Scripture wasn't the only thing that would forever cement my bond with Hardy, however. Over dinner one evening, after a long day on the road spent talking to people about Jesus, Hardy told me he had some photos he wanted to show me of a recent baptism service in Bomi. He'd had the photos made into slides, and after dinner I sat with him in his office where he'd set up a projector to look at the pictures.

The images were of a familiar scene: a half-dozen people being baptized in a river; but one sequence in particular caught my attention. They showed a young woman rising up out of the water after being baptized. She was the most beautiful person I'd ever seen.

I pointed at the screen. "Who is that girl?"

Hardy smiled. "Her name is Elizabeth Fahn."

"Where is she from?"

"She's from Tahn, and she's a former Muslim just like you." Now I was even more excited.

"How can I meet her?"

"You're about to get the chance. I've booked you as one of the speakers this weekend at a conference we're having. Elizabeth should be there."

Little did I realize, my excitement was just the kind of reaction the matchmaking Hardy had been hoping for. When I was introduced to Elizabeth at the conference, I felt a stirring in my heart like none I'd ever felt before. She seemed soft-spoken and kind. We had a lot in common. It was like meeting a longtime friend. More than that, she carried a peace about her that calmed me; it gave me an assurance we were meant to be together.

Elizabeth, whom I'd soon come to call Beth, was from the Gola tribe. Her hometown of village Tahn was in the middle of a prosperous area rich in natural resources: gold, diamonds, and iron ore. These resources had long been mined by foreigners, which made Tahn a place of trade and many coming and goings. The granddaughter of the Muslim village chief, Elizabeth had sought out an education and like me had chosen to place her faith in Jesus Christ. I knew my parents would never approve of her. If being a Christian convert wasn't problematic enough, she was from neither of my parents' tribes, Belle or Mandingo. Still, I was determined to get to know her better. Besides, what did my family's blessing matter now that they had cast me out?

Later that afternoon, Beth and I sat and talked for more than three hours.

"You seem like quite an inspired preacher," she said at one point.

"It isn't me. I'm just a sinner like everyone else."

"Well, sinner or not, you've helped me learn more about Jesus and the Bible."

She told me all about her Gola parents and family, especially her grandmother, who'd had a great influence on her. She told me about her education and how she'd come to accept Jesus. While her Muslim family wasn't happy about her decision, they hadn't outright rejected her the way my family had me.

Beth listened attentively while I poured out my own heart about Belle Balumah, my conversion experience, and my estrangement from my parents. "I'm very sorry. That must be so hard," she said.

Here was a woman who could understand my heart the

way no one else could. I felt like a schoolboy again—completely smitten, even giddy. After only a short time together, it seemed like Elizabeth Fahn knew more about me than anyone else I'd ever met.

The next day, I could hardly wait to get back to Bomi Hills; I immediately went to my desk and composed a handwritten letter to Beth. In it, I poured out my heart, explaining how I would like to start courting her and wanted to marry her. I didn't stop with just a marriage proposal. I outlined my entire vision for our ministry and what our future family and life together as Christians would look like. My letter went on in longhand for more than eight pages. When I finished, I remember thinking that perhaps it was all a bit much for an initial correspondence. Undeterred, I posted the letter and waited.

And waited.

When she failed to promptly respond to my letter, I began to wonder if I had misread God's will. While I kept feeling His assurance that Beth was just the woman for me, maybe God had other ideas when it came to Ms. Elizabeth Fahn.

I still remember standing on the street in Bomi Hills when her reply to my long letter finally did arrive. It was only a small envelope with a card inside containing Beth's polite but brief response to my vainglorious missive:

Thank you for writing to me, Tony. I really enjoyed meeting you.
Sincerely,
Elizabeth Fahn

That was it! That was all!

Stunned, I balled up the envelope and tossed it in the trash. Plunking down on the scooter Hardy had given me, I wiped a tear from my cheek. I was twenty-three years old, a brash young evangelist for Jesus if there ever was one, and I'd just been emotionally smacked as though I'd been struck in the face by a piece of rainforest hardwood. What was God up to? Couldn't he see what I saw? Couldn't he see how committed I was to Jesus?

I'd been so certain Beth was the wife for me. She was the woman who would make all of my dreams come true, and that we would be happy together forever.

Not yet, apparently. Not yet.

***

In 1984, I decided to enroll at African Bible College (ABC) in Yekepa. Nestled in the picturesque Nimba Mountains of Liberia two hundred miles from Monrovia, Yekepa was then an important town, also rich in mining resources, near the border with Guinea. I was offered a scholarship to attend classes and pay the rest of my tuition by working in the college cafeteria. Living in a dormitory with four roommates while receiving the fringe benefit of free food seemed a major luxury, so I jumped at the chance.

ABC would become a very special place to me; as I settled into work and study, I couldn't help but praise God, feeling blessed at the opportunity to further my education at such a wonderful school. While there, I read the complete works of Francis Schaeffer for the first time and was exposed to the works of many other outstanding Christian theologians. Two married couples on faculty had a major influence over me—

Don and Barbara Lentz, who introduced me to the writings of C. S. Lewis, and Barton and Ruth Bliss.

I was constantly asking questions, almost as if a part of me was still uncertain my newfound faith was true. But these professors gently and patiently modeled Christ for me, while at the same time challenging my intellect. ABC became the breeding ground for my future ministry and seminary study in America. Spiritually and intellectually, my time in Yekepa was one of the most productive periods of my life.

My college years were not without heartache, however. While at school, I was shocked to learn my father had unexpectedly died. He'd been such an overpowering figure to me growing up; it was hard to believe he was gone after only a brief illness.

Despite the way he'd sometimes treated me and ultimately disowned me, I felt overcome with grief and sadness. Since Jesus had freed me from my fears, I'd tried on more than one occasion to talk with my father about the forgiveness and freedom to be found in Christ, but he'd refused to even speak with me. I was not invited to attend his Islamic funeral and burial, nor did I participate in the Muslim period of mourning.

I found it difficult to understand my father's unwillingness to even consider what I had to say. Maybe it was his pride. Maybe it was the violence with which he'd grown up. I can't help but believe fear played a role, too; maybe the same fear from which I'd been delivered had somehow overtaken his heart. How I wished I'd had the opportunity to share with him before he died how I'd found a way out.

I turned to the words of Jesus in Matthew 5:4: "Blessed are those who mourn, for they will be comforted."

I also remember a conversation with one of my professors.

"How are you doing, Tony?" he asked. "You haven't seemed yourself lately."

"Still thinking about my father," I admitted.

"Of course. I was very sorry to hear how you lost him."

"It hurts me that he never gave Jesus a chance. Why didn't God open my father's heart to speak with me? Now I will never get the chance."

"I wish I had an easy answer for you," my professor said. "I'm afraid the Holy Spirit doesn't always work in ways we can understand. If it's any comfort, we must remember we can't know everything another person might be thinking or feeling, no matter how well we think we might know them."

"So do you think I'll ever see him again in heaven? I mean, didn't Jesus say, 'I am the way, the truth, and the life, and no man comes to the father but through me'?"

"Jesus did say that. But he also said it's not up to us to judge. Who knows how your belief may have impacted your father? Especially as he was nearing his end."

That gave me some hope, and my mood improved. But I still needed time to grieve. And even at ABC, I couldn't stop dreaming about Beth. I still believed everything I'd written her after we first met. But I'd also come to realize I might have been too overeager and had rushed ahead of whatever plans God might have had for us.

Stopping one rainy morning at the Yekepa post office, I found along with some other correspondence a longer letter from Beth. I felt another stirring in my heart. Was she writing to encourage me in my ministry? Was she writing to finally accept my marriage proposal? Or maybe to tell me she'd married someone else?

Anxiously, I ripped open her letter. Beth wrote that she'd

been thinking and praying for several months about all of the things I'd written. She said she'd considered my proposal carefully because she, too, had felt God's Spirit telling her we were meant to be together. I couldn't believe it! As I continued reading, I was suddenly glad I'd so completely poured myself out to her and made myself vulnerable. My initial letter must have felt like an overload of emotion and information for Beth, but as I read her thoughtful response, it was clear she could handle it and that there was even more to this very special woman than I'd even realized. The prompting I'd felt from the Holy Spirit had been right after all. More than ever, I was convinced Beth was the wife and partner for me, a leader in her own right.

Over the next several months, Beth and I deepened our friendship through correspondence; I poured my heart out to her again and again. During my final two years of college, we started dating. Whenever I could, I would travel from Yekepa to Bomi Hills where she lived. Before too long, I met some of Beth's family members. As they'd accepted Beth's conversion from Islam to Christianity, so they also accepted me and my desire to be a pastor.

"You're impossible," Beth told me one day. "But I think I'm falling in love with you anyway."

"So that means you'll marry me?"

"Yes, Tony. We can move ahead with plans."

"Yes!"

I nearly leapt into the air, and my soul soared as we embraced. After that, our correspondence and times together took on a renewed urgency. I traveled to Tahn more than once to get to know her Gola parents better. A few months later, despite the continued schism between my family and me, I took Beth to my home village to meet them. Even with my father gone, it was an important African custom to seek my family's approval of my future bride; we even took Hardy with us for the first couple of days as a sort of chaperone.

Mama acted outwardly polite toward me, but I sensed coolness in her demeanor, and our interactions were awkward. No doubt she still felt badly wounded by me. Not only had I become a Christian, but I was planning to marry another former Muslim to boot. If Mama could reject her own son, she was not likely to accept a young woman who was also an apostate from Islam. It might have helped if Beth were from the same tribe as either of my parents, which of course Beth wasn't.

Hardy did his best to smooth things over with everyone, but despite Beth's love for me, I could tell that after meeting Mama, she was having doubts about marrying into my family.

"I don't know, Tony. I really do love you and feel God has brought us together, but—" she confessed to me after a particularly terse exchange with Mama. As per custom for the intended bride, Beth had cooked a meal for the entire family. All who ate said they were impressed at how good the food was, except Mama. Her demeanor telegraphed that her disapproval wasn't about to be bought off by food.

After Hardy left, the tension came to a head the next day when Beth asked me if I would take her to visit the cemetery where my father, grandparents, and other family members were buried near the center of town. I remember thinking it was an odd request. "You really want to go visit our family cemetery while you're here?"

"Yes. Of course."

I wondered if maybe this was Beth's way of attempting to

honor our family and impress her future mother-in-law. "All right. If you insist."

My ancestors had helped found Balumah and been leaders of the village, so their graves were carefully arranged in a place of honor beneath the shade of a large cotton tree. I'd enjoyed spending time here as a child. Somehow, the grave markers gave me comfort and reassurance that I wasn't alone in the world; I'd come from an important family.

Beth beamed and chattered with excitement as we approached the site. I looked at her, confused. "What's going on with you? Why are you so happy?"

"You have a family cemetery!" Beth said. "That's so wonderful!"

I enjoyed the place, but I really didn't see what was quite so exciting about visiting our family graves.

"Don't you see?" Beth went on. "Your father is from the Belle tribe."

"So?"

"My father and mother have been trying to convince me people from the Belle tribe eat their dead."

"Eat our dead? What in the world are you talking about?"

Apparently, mine wasn't the only family having misgivings about accepting a new in-law from a different tribe! Beth must have really been worried because, after we had a good laugh together, she couldn't stop smiling.

***

Beyond our family tensions and concerns, turmoil was also beginning to boil again across Liberia. After the initial jubilation over the ouster of the America-Liberian government, the new Doe government's policies, especially Doe's favoritism toward his fellow Krahn tribesmen and persecution of others, began to have a corrosive effect on national unity. Classmates of mine from Yekepa warned me that "heavy rain" was coming. By this they meant some sort of uprising or fighting led by anti-Doe rebels from the Nimba mountain region where Yekepa was located.

It had been nearly three years since Doe had finally restored the constitution and gotten himself elected president through what many outside observers pegged as a fraudulent voting process. In November, the former commander of Doe's military, who was from the Mano tribe in Nimba, led a number of rebel army units, many of them also Mano tribesmen, in an attempt to overthrow Doe. The Nimba region sits just across the border from the neighboring Ivory Coast. The rebels attempted to infiltrate the rest of the country and the capital of Monrovia from there; they even briefly seized control of the ELWA radio station (where their broadcast pronouncements briefly sent people dancing in the streets), but most of the rebels were soon killed, and the coup attempt ultimately failed.

Since Yekepa was the central city in the Nimba region, hundreds of Doe's soldiers soon arrived in Yekepa to quell any more ideas of rebellion. Our Africa Bible College campus was spared, but Doe's men arrested and executed many men from the Mano tribe. One of those killed was the brother-in-law of Charles Taylor, a former member of Doe's cabinet, who'd fled the country after being accused of embezzlement. This particular killing would one day come back to haunt President Doe in ways no one then could imagine. As traumatic as these events were, yet more horror was on the horizon.

George and Libby Senter were longtime Baptist missionaries living in Yekepa. They had a ten-year-old daughter named Rachel. George Senter pastored a church in Yekepa, and the Senters had been primarily responsible for translating the Bible into the Mano language. A native Liberian named Benjamin Morris had recently come to work for the Senters' church as an associate pastor.

In late November 1986, George Senter traveled to Monrovia to pick up the Senters' older son Philip, who was coming home for the Thanksgiving holiday. It was an overnight trip, and while George was away, Benjamin Morris, no stranger in the Senter home, attacked and stabbed to death Libby Senter and their daughter Rachel before disappearing into the night.

The bodies weren't discovered until the next morning. The local Christian community and those of us at the Bible College were in shock. How could such a thing have happened? Yekepa was a company town controlled by the Liberian American Mining Company. Instead of city police, there was a company police force. An investigation was undertaken, and Benjamin Morris was eventually taken into custody trying to sneak across the border in stolen clothes. Morris was eventually tried and convicted and sentenced to life in prison for his crime. But that did little in the Nimba region to quell the anxiety.

Many worried that the executions and murder in Yekepa were but a foreshadowing of more widespread terrors to come. Fear hung in the air like a cancer across Liberia. War, or something like it, only seemed to be awaiting the right mixture of oppression with a spark, a demonic fire lying somewhere over the horizon.

CHAPTER SIXTEEN

Books

In April 2004, I walked back into our Denver apartment to see that the boxes we'd shipped from Ethiopia had finally arrived. I set my suitcase on the floor, having just returned from days of meetings at SIM headquarters in North Carolina. A note from Beth on the lampstand explained she was out running errands, the kids were in school, and our boxes had arrived earlier that morning; she wrote she hadn't had time to open them before she left.

I took a moment to shed my coat. The temperature outside was barely above freezing, and the warmth of the apartment felt good. I was exhausted from traveling but curious about the boxes. In our experience, things shipped from Africa didn't always arrive intact, if at all. While we'd have preferred to bring all our belongings with us when we moved from Ethiopia back to the United States, we'd been overloaded with four children and many other containers. So we'd found a shipper who'd promised to deliver these remaining boxes for far less than it would cost to have them flown with us.

The weathered, tightly taped cardboard containers filled our tiny hallway like a stack of hay bales. A delivery receipt was attached to one of the boxes, and immediately I noticed a problem. We'd shipped seven boxes from Ethiopia. According to the delivery manifest, there were only six in this shipment.

I'd helped Beth pack each box, so I had a good idea of what was in them—clothing, kitchen utensils, and other sundry items as well as a number of my books. I sighed, wondering which one of the boxes might be missing. Retrieving a pair of scissors, I cut them open and set to work inventorying the contents.

It didn't take long before I realized which box was missing—the one containing my theology books, specifically my collection of the complete works of Francis Schaeffer. Everything else was replaceable, but these books held a particular significance in my heart and mind. I made several phone calls to the shipping company over the next couple of weeks, attempting to track down the missing box.

Beth placed a comforting hand on my shoulder as I listened to the final word on the subject in broken English from a clerk in Addis Ababa. "I'm sorry, sir. It seems like the box with your book is just lost."

"Books," I corrected. "Not just one book. There are many."

"Yes, sir, I'm sorry, sir. The box with your books is gone."

CHAPTER SEVENTEEN

A Curious Wedding

After graduating from Africa Bible College in 1987, I returned to Monrovia to continue my ministry as an evangelist and look for other work. Beth and I had set a date for our wedding, and I traveled regularly to see her in Bomi Hills. I'd also become a familiar face around the ELWA radio compound. Hardy provided me with a glowing employment reference as did Pauline Sonius, and I was soon hired by SIM International, the parent missionary organization that operated ELWA radio in Liberia.

Sudan Interior Mission (now SIM) was one of the oldest Western missionary organizations operating in Liberia, founded in 1893 through the vision of Canadians Walter Gowans and Roland Bingham, and American Thomas Kent, three ground-breaking young men willing to go where no established mission agencies at that time had gone. SIM had been sharing the gospel of Jesus Christ in sub-Saharan Africa ever since.

ELWA operated the largest radio broadcasting facility in Africa with a signal that reached throughout Liberia as well as into the neighboring countries of Guinea, the Ivory Coast, and Sierra Leone, and even as far as the Middle East. The ELWA campus at that time housed nearly two hundred missionaries and support personnel. The ELWA hospital was the best run and equipped medical facility in Liberia with a well-trained staff of doctors and nurses. ELWA Academy, a private school for the children of foreign missionaries, embassy staff, and other expatriates, had an enrollment of over 150 students.

As a native Liberian college graduate and former Muslim, I was hired to serve as SIM's director of Muslim ministries in West Africa. The job included radio programming and evangelistic outreach material for the Liberian Mandingo community and the Muslim Mandinka peoples in neighboring countries.

ELWA stands for Eternal Love Winning Africa. Broadcasting on FM 94.5 and SW 4760 kHz (60 meters) with a transmission power of 1,000 watts (1 kilowatt), the station had been offering Christian programming and music since 1954. Radio was the dominant media throughout Africa. Since ELWA was an independent broadcaster—as opposed to the propaganda and bias of government-controlled radio stations—a majority of Liberians and even those beyond Liberia's borders had come to depend on ELWA as their predominant source of accurate local information. Most also listened nightly to the BBC, but it carried only major African news stories along with other international news.

In addition to my radio programming on ELWA, I also wrote a regular column on religion for Liberia's largest newspaper. I became a recognizable public figure witnessing about Jesus's love and my conversion from Islam. Being the son of a Mandingo mother, I was also asked to travel to Guinea to help counsel and translate for SIM missionaries working there among the Mandinka.

"I wish you would just go away and be quiet," Mama told me on one of the rare occasions in which we made contact. "I'm glad your father isn't alive to see this. I don't know what would've happened."

The implication was that he or one of our other relatives might have resorted to violence in order to silence me.

Since I spoke several Liberian tribal dialects, my job included helping expatriate SIM missionaries working throughout the country better understand and integrate into the different tribal communities. For me, working with SIM and ELWA was in many ways the opportunity of a lifetime, especially since well-paid work was becoming harder and harder to come by for native Liberians under Doe's dysfunctional and egomaniacal government.

I wish I could say my life was free of all cares and concerns, but it wasn't: Mama's words and my family's rejection still haunted me at times. I also learned that, even within the safe confines of our missionary community, tensions existed that in some ways mirrored our country's historic divides between Americo-Liberians and native Liberians. ELWA's campus had a beautiful beachfront where the foreign missionaries, who were almost all white, lived in comparatively luxurious houses on the white sandy beachside with the cool ocean air blowing away mosquitoes and bad smells. Meanwhile, we native African staff were relegated to smaller homes in less salubrious, swampy areas next to the radio broadcasting towers or across the main road outside of the compound altogether.

"Sometimes I think it's like little Soweto," one of the other African ELWA staff members joked to me under his breath one morning as we worked together on a project.

We watched through the window as the well dressed, happy children of expatriate ELWA missionaries headed off to school at the ELWA Academy. Because there wasn't enough room at the ELWA campus, I knew some of the staff members' children were forced to live with relatives in the city.

I understood his reference to the infamous South African ghetto in Johannesburg where, under apartheid, blacks were segregated from whites. His comments reflected a general frustration with the way things were—even within the missionary community. I loved all of my brothers and sisters in Christ of different races, many of whom had come from other countries and given up easier lives elsewhere to work here, but seeing such things made me sad.

Meanwhile, my estrangement with Mama and my other family members deepened. I continued to study the Bible and pray each day. When doubts crept in, I would find myself wrestling with God like Jacob in Genesis 32, crying out for clarity and peace, trying to understand how God was continuing to work even when I couldn't make sense of His will.

Sometimes I was stalked by guilt about Mama's anger and grief. Sometimes the pain of family isolation seemed like too much to bear. I even tried to build myself up at times by imagining the embarrassment and pain I might be causing my other family members, like Uncle Sekou. I'd continued to reach out to them about Jesus, but so far to no avail.

If had to choose between God and my family, there was really no choice at all. I had to obey God. I had my heavenly Father, Jesus, and the Holy Spirit to turn to, and soon I would have my wife. Even so, the specter of shame and emotional pain from being shunned by my family still haunted me sometimes, like a dark cloud attempting to undermine my faith. I was learning that, even when Jesus frees us from our fears, removing those shackles isn't like pressing a button to receive your drink from a vending machine. Only by continuing to pray and study His word can we learn to rest in our faith in order to fully experience and embrace the freedom Jesus brings.

***

All was going according to plan for our wedding until I received a letter from Mama one day while Beth and I were out running errands in preparation for the upcoming ceremony. Standing outside the Monrovia post office with the letter in my hands, I had to reread it more than once before the words sunk in. Beth burst into tears as she read the letter alongside me. Mama was refusing to come to our wedding.

In the African tradition, where a wedding represents not just the union of two people but the joining and mutual honoring of two families, Mama's refusal to attend our Christian ceremony represented a huge affront to Beth's family, especially her father. Was my family attempting to sabotage our getting married? Even though Beth's family was also Muslim, they'd consented to our marriage as Christians. Not only that, Beth's family had already sent out invitations and an announcement about the wedding in the Christian church in Beth's hometown of Tahn.

The small church there was still fairly new. Ours would be the first Christian wedding ever held in Tahn, and we'd heard that many of the Muslims from the area were curious and even interested in coming. Mama's letter put all of our hopes for our wedding ceremony in jeopardy.

"If Tony's mother doesn't agree to come to the wedding," Beth's father told her, "then that must mean Tony's family is rejecting you as his wife. This marriage cannot take place."

I was at a loss about what to do, but Beth had an idea.

"Why don't you go talk to your Uncle Tommy?" she suggested "Isn't his wife Sarta from the Gola tribe like me?"

"That's a great idea," I said. "Mama has always had a soft spot in her heart for Uncle Tommy."

Tommy, being the youngest of Mama's siblings, had always been loved and doted upon by Mama and my older aunts. Off I went to Bomi Hills, back to the home where Tommy and his wife Sarta had taken me in to help advance my schooling so many years before.

Arriving at their house, I saw my aunt and uncle seated together on a bench out front talking. To my relief, their eyes lit up when they caught sight of me.

"Tony! It's so good to see you. We've heard about your upcoming wedding. A chieftain's granddaughter you're marrying. This Elizabeth Fahn. Congratulations!"

"Actually, that's the reason I've come to see you today. It's about the wedding."

I went on to tell them about the letter I'd received from Mama.

"She what!?" Uncle Tommy exclaimed. "My sister is refusing to come to your wedding? That's not right."

I shook my head and shrugged.

"You let me talk to your mama. Maybe she just needs some reassurance that marrying a Gola woman is not so bad as she thinks," Uncle Tommy said, winking at Sarta.

"Not so bad!" Sarta punched him playfully in the arm. "You better tell Tony's mama it's more than not so bad. You need to make sure this marriage between Tony and his girl Beth, the chieftain's granddaughter, goes forward."

"I will, woman. And don't you worry, Tony. I will deal with your mother."

***

Despite our fears, Beth and I continued moving forward with plans for our wedding. To our great relief, when the day arrived, Mama actually did show up. I don't know exactly what Uncle Tommy said to Mama, but whatever it was, it worked.

As the ceremony was underway, Mama sat dutifully along with my older sister MJ across from Beth's family in one of the front pews. To our amazement, the church was packed with family and well-wishers with over five hundred people in attendance. Many others, mostly curious Mandingo Muslims, stood outside peering into the windows. Everyone in town apparently wanted to have a look at this man who was marrying the chieftain's beautiful granddaughter.

Standing by the altar at the front of the church, I could feel tears running down my face as Beth in her wedding attire approached me. She looked radiant, and I felt radiant as Beth's pastor, James Varney, pronounced our vows. "Do you, Tony, take this woman, Beth? … Do you, Beth, take this man, Tony?"

The power of the Holy Spirit was as clearly manifest to me as it ever has been. Beth's family was very generous and paid for everything. Many of my classmates and friends from African Bible College also attended, which made for quite a joyous celebration following the wedding. Throughout the ceremony and festivities that followed, Mama didn't look at all happy, but Beth and I still appreciated that she'd at least put in an appearance. MJ later told me Mama had said to her, "Our son is a rebel who is lost, but we go to show respect for the family name."

CHAPTER EIGHTEEN

Live Through the Night

Mama and most of the rest of my family would miss the miracle that rescued our newborn daughter from death. Beth became pregnant not long after we were married. My work with SIM was going well, and we were both excited to be expecting our first child. Unfortunately, once our wedding was past, Mama stopped responding to any of my letters or attempts to reach out to her, so she wasn't there when our daughter Abigail was born.

After we'd taken Abigail home from the hospital, everything seemed fine until one day Abigail began to struggle for breath. We rushed her to the doctor, and she was admitted to the ELWA hospital and diagnosed with staphylococcus pneumonia.

We watched anxiously as our little baby was hooked to tubes and blood cultures were drawn, her tiny body and miniscule blood vessels making it difficult for the doctors to provide the desperately needed care. We cried out to God on her behalf, along with our many missionary and church friends who lifted her up in prayer, yet nothing seemed to be working. Abigail didn't respond to the treatment. I remember leaning against the wall outside her hospital room a couple of days after Abigail had been admitted, feeling overcome with grief. Beth was beside me as a doctor spoke to us in a soft, compassionate voice. He explained apologetically that they'd done all they could medically for our baby girl and that it looked as though the end for her was near.

Why would God want to take our baby? Were we being punished somehow? As a Christian, I knew this wasn't true, but it was hard not to succumb to the fears instilled in me from childhood by my parents and native culture. What else could we do but offer Abigail's broken little body up to the Lord?

As Abigail's condition worsened, Beth's family had wanted us to take her out of the ELWA hospital and bring her to an herbalist, whom they were convinced was the only one who could save our child, but we refused. Sadly, the doctor informed us our baby might not live through the night.

Mama and my family—and even some of Beth's family too—might well see in Abigail's illness and imminent death Allah's judgment against Beth and me for converting to Christianity and choosing to marry. While our many Christian friends and a few of the medical staff still held out hope for healing, in my darkest moments I couldn't help but wonder if Mama was somehow right to have never recognized the validity of my marriage to Beth.

Utterly exhausted and unable to think straight, Beth and I clung to one another in the hallway. Together we cried out to Jesus to save us from every parent's worst nightmare—the loss of a child.

"Go home and rest," the doctor said. "There's nothing more

you can do for your baby right now, and you two are in desperate need of sleep."

"But what if she dies?"

"Don't worry," he assured us. "We'll call you when it looks like the absolute end."

We left the hospital in shock and grief, praying and still hoping against hope for a miracle, yet relinquishing all control, leaving her life up to God. At least we could be there when our daughter died, we reasoned. At least we could hold our baby daughter's hand and sing her to sleep one last time.

When the phone woke us a few hours later at the house where we were staying, I felt sick at heart. I knew it had to be the doctor or one of the nurses calling to tell us to hurry back because the end was near. Instead, I heard the voice of one of the many SIM missionaries who'd been there supporting us and praying for us.

"Tell Beth to hurry up and get back down here to the hospital," she said. "Your baby Abigail is hungry. She needs to be fed."

"What?" I rubbed the sleep from my eyes. Was I having a dream? "But she's dying."

"Not anymore. She crying at the top of lungs. She needs her mother's milk."

Beth didn't believe it was true. "They're just trying to make her passing easier on us, Tony. Don't you see?"

We raced back down to the hospital.

I will never forget the moment we stepped back into Abigail's hospital room to find a circle of smiling faces. Virtually every doctor, nurse, and missionary who'd prayed for us and helped provide care for Abigail had come together to see the miracle God had performed.

Beautiful, tiny Abigail still lay in the same small crib where we'd left her so gravely ill just a few hours before, but her breathing tube was gone. So were the other hoses, needles, and other life support connections that had been keeping her alive. Miracle of miracles—Abigail was now breathing normally. In fact, just as the missionary had told me on the phone, our baby was screaming for the comfort of Beth's arms and nourishment.

CHAPTER NINETEEN

Terrified

Late one night in May 2004, Beth and I sat in the kitchen of our Denver apartment with a stony silence between us.

The children had all gone to bed. The windows and doors stood open to the outdoors. This was something I'd come to appreciate about Colorado: in the late spring and early summer, the chill mountain air flows down to cool the city, and unlike many other places we'd lived, we felt safe enough to leave the door and windows open after dark.

Beth went to the stove and picked up a teapot we'd brought back with us from Africa. Walking back, she poured more hot tea into my mug.

"Thank you," I said.

"You're welcome." Her tone was even cooler than the air flowing in from outside. We'd been back in America for a few months now, and while things were okay on the surface, I'd sensed a growing tension between us. I had a busy speaking schedule and was still trying to work out some of the details of my new position with SIM as director of Muslim ministries.

Beth had her own work issues, but those weren't the source of our tension. Since getting off the flight from Ethiopia, we'd continued talking off and on about my hope to return to Liberia to find Mama; Beth was still very much opposed.

She reached across the table and put her hand on mine.

"Tony Weedor, do you even know what you are doing?"

"What?" The question caught me off guard.

"Do you even know what you are doing about your mother and talk about going back to Liberia?"

"I hope I do, yes."

"I think you might be getting ahead of God."

"Ahead of God?"

"This is your life you're gambling with. Our life and our future together. Maybe even our children's lives. Can't you see, Tony? The kids and I are terrified."

"What do you mean *terrified*?"

I knew our kids were dealing with some anxiety like Abigail had told me, but overall I thought they were mostly excited to be back in America from Addis Ababa.

"They're too afraid to even talk to you about it anymore," she said. "We're all terrified about the potential of losing you."

"No one's losing anybody," I said.

"How do you know? Can you guarantee me that?"

I said nothing.

"Besides, you already have your work cut out for you back here," Beth went on. "You had two more calls about speaking engagements just this week. People in the churches all want to hear from you about Islam, especially with everything that's going on in the world with terrorism. Why would you want to go back to Liberia now? Your mother has rejected you. Your whole family has rejected you—and they've rejected me."

"I know. I'm so sorry. But how can I tell people what it was like growing up Muslim and meeting Jesus when my own Muslim mother may be suffering? I can't fully explain why I feel the way I do."

"Well, maybe you should start trying to explain it, Tony, and search your heart. I've been in touch with some of my family outside Monrovia. They tell me things are still very dangerous there. What if something happens? What if you die or disappear ...? And where will you get money to pay for the trip? You know we don't have it."

She was right. I had no answer for any of her questions.

An even deeper silence descended on the room. My tea sat untouched, growing cold.

Beth's demeanor softened. "Look," she suggested, "Why don't you wait a year or two? Maybe the situation in Liberia will have improved by then."

"Maybe." I was tired after a long day of work and tired of talking about this subject. I folded my arms across my chest.

"You say *maybe*," she said. "But I know you, Tony Weedor. Unless God stops you, you're going to keep trying to find a way to go."

I grew angry then and said something I would later regret about Beth getting in my way and getting in the way of God. She glared at me across the kitchen table as if I'd struck her with the back of my hand. Pushing away from the table, she rose to her feet and stalked into our bedroom, slamming the door behind her.

CHAPTER TWENTY

From a Distance

The last time I'd laid eyes on my mother was in 1989.

I'd flown into my home village of Belle Balumah on a P-130 military aircraft to speak at a ceremony sponsored by Wycliffe Bible Translators in celebration of their translation of the Bible into the Belle language.

I watched the rainforest canopy open up as we came in for a landing on the grass runway to which I'd once been brought gravely ill from Monrovia. The small airstrip continued to serve as the only direct transportation connection to the outside world. The only other way to get to Balumah was via forest trails and, for a brief period of time, a temporary logging road cut by a lumber company. Travel over that route was often hazardous, however, and sometimes nonexistent, depending on the amount of rain and the condition of the road. Despite these many obstacles, Wycliffe missionaries in the area had managed to finish their translation of the English Bible into Belle, and had asked me to say a few words to honor the occasion. I was also secretly hoping I might get to speak with Mama.

Unfortunately, my spirit sagged as I stepped out of the plane and saw that none of my family was there to greet me.

Apparently, Uncle Sekou, Mama, and most of my other family members still saw my Christian faith as a personal affront, so I wasn't expecting them to be happy about the Bible translation. Still, a part of me had hoped, perhaps naively, that Mama at least might show up to greet me upon my arrival.

Maybe the Bible translation didn't even mean that much to my family. Ours was an oral Muslim tradition, and so were most of the teachings. My Uncle Sekou was even proud of his difficulties reading and writing. He'd received his Islamic training directly from the spoken words of the previous imam. This was considered a badge of honor of sorts since Muhammad himself was said to have been illiterate, teaching in the oral tradition and passing on the words of the Quran to scribes, who then wrote them down.

The outdoor ceremony was to be a brief one. A number of missionaries had gathered at the end of the village's grass runway along with a few dozen Christians from the surrounding area. Since I was raised here and spoke Belle, I'd been asked to say a few words in both Belle and English about the significance of the Bible translation into my native language. The importance of this accomplishment wasn't lost on me. While English was our country's official language, we'd looked upon it when I was growing up as the "Americo-Liberian" and "foreign white man's" language. Perhaps if I had been exposed to the Bible in a language other than English, I might have come to accept Jesus earlier, and others might have as well.

When the ceremony began, our Wycliffe hosts made introductions and the local missionaries said a few words. They then introduced me as the speaker. I spoke for a few minutes, and did my best to offer a personal word of thanks and an encouragement to the gathered group. Soon thereafter, the ceremony began drawing toward a close. I'd been warned by the Bible translators not to try to go after Mama or drag her into our celebration. We wanted to respect her feelings and those of the other Muslims.

The ceremony was nearly over before I caught sight of Mama. I could make out her familiar figure among a group of Muslim women observing from a distance. She wouldn't come near the ceremony, of course, but maybe she'd heard I'd be speaking.

There was so much I wanted to share with her about my life and work at ELWA, about how things were going with my marriage, and about Beth. I also wanted to ask how she and the rest of the family were doing. How were my brothers and sisters? How was Mama faring with her business and the farm? I feared she was still angry with me due to my continued public presence on the radio and in the newspaper as a Christian missionary working with foreigners.

As the event was finishing up, I finally made eye contact from a distance with Mama. I knew she saw me. It only lasted for a moment, however, before she turned away, and my stomach twisted in sadness as she disappeared back into the village.

CHAPTER TWENTY-ONE

Make Clear

After my argument with Beth in our apartment kitchen, I drove early the next morning to the Denver seminary library in Englewood to study the Bible and pray. I hadn't slept well; I felt guilty about the harsh words I'd spoken to Beth the night before. I saw Beth before I left, but she ignored me. I imagined she was angry. Spending time with books, I hoped, would comfort me as it had always done.

Reaching the library, I found a quiet corner among the long stacks of books. The familiar smell of old bound books and wood shelving took me back to my seminary days. What a difference theological volumes like these had made in my life. A love for learning had been a constant in my life since childhood.

Sitting there among so many thousands of words on biblical scholarship, I asked myself some blunt questions. Why did I feel such a calling in my spirit to return to Liberia? Why should I even try to reconnect with Mama at all?

Maybe Beth was right. She was certainly right about our not having the money to fund such a trip.

"God," I prayed, "if you've put this desire in my heart for a reason, please show me the way. If you want me to go, I'll go. If not, I'll stay. Either way, I trust you, Lord. I'll wait for you to make the path clear."

By the time I returned to the sidewalk outside, I had begun to feel a little better. Clouds had formed overhead, and a cool, steady rain had begun to fall. I'd been thinking I might invite Beth to go on a picnic to try to make up with her, but maybe the picnic would have to wait.

"Tony? Tony Weedor?"

I looked up to see a man about my age approaching from the parking lot. Caucasian. Tall. "Bentley?"

"Yeah, it's me," he grinned.

"Bentley Tate! I can't believe it! So good to see you, brother!" We shook hands, then embraced, laughing.

"Good to see you, too!" he said. "What are you doing here? Last I heard, you and your family were in Ethiopia."

Bentley Tate was a medical doctor, specifically a specialist in emergency medicine. He'd also been a friend of mine since we were at Denver Seminary together ten years earlier. He was an extraordinary individual who'd already completed his medical training before choosing to go to seminary. In addition to his emergency room practice, he'd wanted to serve on regular short-term medical missions and felt he could more effectively meet both the medical and spiritual needs of his patients by adding pastoral training to his resume.

Bentley and I had spent a good deal of time together while in seminary but hadn't seen one another in years. For the next half an hour, we stood in the rain under an awning outside the library and caught up on each other's lives.

We talked about our wives and children. He listened while I told him about our work with SIM in Ethiopia, and he told me about his own medical missionary work.

After seminary, he'd completed training at the London School of Tropical Medicine. While continuing his full-time work as an emergency room physician in Colorado, he had undertaken a number of medical mission projects over the past few years. Recently he'd cofounded a medical missionary organization caring for children in orphanages in Myanmar called Asia Heartbeat.

After a while, the conversation waned, and Bentley looked me in the eye. "If you don't mind me saying, something seems to be troubling you, my friend."

I forced a sad smile. "Is it so obvious?"

Looking out at the rain, I confessed to him my reason for being at the library that morning. I told him about the argument I'd had with Beth the night before. I told him about my hope to try to reunite with Mama. We talked about Liberia and how dangerous things were there now.

He listened some more and then asked, "What's the current State Department recommendation about traveling to Liberia?"

"Not to travel."

"And it sounds like with good reason. Beth loves you, Tony. Of course she's scared for you to go alone."

"I know."

Together we stared out at the rain coming down from underneath our awning.

Bentley suddenly spoke up.

"You know what? How about if I go with you to Liberia?"

I stared at him. "What?"

"I'll go with you. I can be your wingman."

"Are you kidding?"

"No. Not about something like this."

"You're serious."

"Yes. You and I can go together."

"Aren't you worried about what might happen?"

"Yes, but I've been on mission trips like this before."

I was stunned, but suddenly hopeful. "That would be amazing! It would be so much safer to have you with me."

I paused, my words trailing off into the sound of the rain as I remembered the cost of travel.

"I'm sorry, Bentley," I admitted. "I really appreciate your offer but I don't have the money to pay for such a trip."

"Money? If that's all that's holding you back, don't worry. I can take care of that, too."

I was dumbfounded. The suddenness of it all—this chance encounter with Bentley—it was an offer of so much grace. I found myself beaming from ear to ear while tears were streaming down my face. "I don't know what to say. I can't thank you enough. I can't believe this is happening. God is so amazing."

"You don't have to say anything," Bentley said gently. "We'll go together in Jesus' name."

"Yes, my friend."

"When do you want to leave?"

"Soon," I said.

Before traveling back to Liberia to try to make peace with my mother, I needed to drive back home to our apartment to make peace with my wife.

CHAPTER TWENTY-TWO

Nightmare-Ville

Two weeks after my surprise encounter with Bentley, the captain's voice crackled through the overhead speakers to inform us that our Brussels Air 747, inbound from our stopover in Abidjan, Ivory Coast, was about to arrive in Monrovia.

I was struck by the routine tone of the pilot's voice. Weary, yet measured. Melancholy perhaps. As if this was simply one more trip, no different than other commercial flights he'd piloted. As if we all weren't about to enter—despite a fragile UN-imposed and managed peace—a war zone. As if my life wasn't about to cross a threshold not just to potential physical danger, but spiritual and emotional danger as well.

I looked out the cabin window, hoping to glimpse the familiar coastline of my homeland, but it was long after dark and raining, and all I could see outside was the glowing-red navigation light on the plane's wingtip slipping through murk and mist.

The date was May 31, 2004. Back in Colorado, people were firing up their outdoor grills, drinking beer, watching baseball on TV, and maybe opening up their swimming pools to enjoy the final celebrations of Memorial Day weekend. Here, those pleasantries added up to little more than an alternative reality, a reality that for me at least during the next few days would cease to exist.

Since my chance meeting with Bentley outside the seminary library, I'd practically memorized the State Department warnings about traveling in Liberia. Don't travel in the city at night. Don't venture at all into the country's interior. I'd watched the BBC news reports about what had been happening in Monrovia over the past several months. The shelling of the city the summer before had made a bad situation worse. Teenage gunmen and even armed children had roamed the streets, forcing the UN to intervene to put a stop to the killing. A forced halt in widespread fighting only put a bandage over a gaping wound.

Still, I was thankful to be on this trip and to have Bentley with me. If worse came to worst, at least I had an emergency physician on my side.

The huge jet pushed through turbulence as we descended, and the wind kicked droplets of rain against the outside glass. When we finally broke through the cloud cover, I caught my first shadowy glimpse of land below. Up ahead, the bright landing lights of Monrovia Roberts International Airport pierced the darkness.

Even though Roberts Airport was nearly thirty miles outside the capital, with its ten-thousand-foot runway built by the American military, it had once been a proud, prosperous hub for international flights going in and out of Africa. At the time, the runway even served as an alternative emergency landing site for the NASA space shuttle. NASA would never dream of trying to land a space shuttle here now. We were lucky to still be able to fly in on our huge jetliner.

Beyond the airport, all I could see was the inky darkness of the jungle. As the plane settled into its landing, it shuddered and swayed until our tires touched down on the wet pavement. After breaking into a slow taxi, a chime sounded, and one of the Belgian stewardesses announced in cheery English, "Welcome to Monrovia! The local time is—"

This was followed by a canned arrival message. We could almost be touching down in London or Tokyo with our choice of connecting flights or ground transportation to some comfortable hotel, I thought, until I heard a man seated a few rows in front of us among a group laden with cameras and other equipment mutter, "Sure. Welcome to Nightmare-ville!"

The plane slowly pivoted toward the poorly lit terminal. I glanced around at the other passengers. They looked to be a mixture of aid workers, UN staff, and military personnel. Most appeared pale and bone-weary. Everyone seemed wary.

The airport had no doubt been a strategic location during the civil wars. As we rolled along the runway, I searched through the haze of light and fog for any familiar signs. All I could make out were the shadowy silhouettes of palm trees surrounding the runway. Soon the gutted shell of the old main airport building came into view.

Growing up, I remembered my father speaking with pride about what was then one of the most modern terminals in all of Africa. Now all that remained of its former glory were pockmarked concrete pillars holding up the exoskeleton of blackened walls and a burned-out roof, a ghostly reminder of the fighting that had taken place here.

Between the old terminal and a cargo building that had been converted to accept arriving flights sat several military aircraft and helicopter gunships backed by klieg lights, looking like huge robot reptiles with slanted windshields for eyes. African men in military uniforms with the blue helmets signifying they were UN peacekeepers were mustering into formation, making a line on the tarmac next to a recently arrived cargo plane. The soldiers carried large backpacks and automatic rifles.

Other military personnel were busy offloading equipment, arms, and armored vehicles. They were all part of a massive UN peacekeeping effort known as UNMIL (United Nations Mission in Liberia) established less than a year before. Over 15,000 UN troops now occupied the country and were in control of most of it.

The jetliner lurched to a stop. Another chime sounded as the cabin lights flickered on and the captain turned off the seatbelt signs. Throughout the plane, people began to rise and gather up their things, but I stayed in my seat staring out the window. Though the rain had stopped, huge sheets of water still coated the tarmac. A crew of men in orange airport vests was wheeling a tall set of air stairs into position at the side of the plane.

Suddenly, the pilot's voice emerged again from the overhead speakers to announce that there would be a delay in opening the cabin door due to a UN security check. His words were greeted with weary groans all around. I reached for my cell phone, then remembered there was no point turning it on here. The electrical grid had been destroyed, and except for a few scattered generators, Liberia at night was now a country cloaked in darkness.

First Bullets

The trouble for Beth and me began in Monrovia on the second anniversary of our wedding. It was July 2, 1990, a cloud-filled, rainy morning but with patches of beautiful blue sky overhead. I laughed with delight as Beth kissed me awake.

"Happy anniversary, my husband."

"Happy anniversary to you too, Mrs. Weedor."

"Are you sure you have to go to work today?" she asked. In the next room, Abigail, now a little over a year old, stirred awake in her crib, cooing and laughing.

"Yes, honey. I'm sorry, but they need me there."

"I'm worried you won't be safe. I've heard there's been fighting nearby."

"We'll be fine," I assured her.

The fighting had been going on for more than six months. Charles Taylor, Doe's former finance manager whose brother-in-law had been executed by Doe's forces in Yekepa, had returned from exile to the Ivory Coast, where he'd raised a rebel army of discontented Liberians with the support and guidance of Libya's Muammar Gaddafi. Calling itself the National Patriotic Front of Liberia (NPFL), this army crossed over the border from the Ivory Coast into the Nimba region on Christmas Eve 1989, initiating Liberia's first civil war. The fighting between Doe's Liberian Army troops and Charles Taylor's NPFL rebels had been raging ever since in much of the interior of the country. But in Monrovia and its surrounding suburbs, the fighting seemed far away. Ordinary people went to work or opened their shops or businesses each morning as though we in the capital were immune to the violence. We felt sure the civil war was confined to other regions of the country and we at least were safe.

To many of us by that time, Doe and his brutal government had been in control of Liberia for so long they seemed too entrenched for any likelihood of rebels overrunning Monrovia. President Doe spent much of his time in his heavily fortified executive mansion. He was even rumored to have employed specially trained Israeli troops who had at their disposal long-range mortars and rockets as well as other high-tech weapons. Just the weekend before, the president had staged a lavish festival in the city to celebrate his birthday.

On occasion, alarming news would reach our ears via the BBC as well as through various reports from SIM missionaries located elsewhere in Liberia. But communication with friends and family in other parts of the country remained difficult, if not impossible. For regular Liberian civilians such as us, as well as the many expatriate Christian missionaries with whom Beth and I worked, there was really no way to discern what was going on beyond our immediate area. As the months wore on, we learned that some rebel forces had fought their way to the suburbs of Monrovia and that battles were occurring just a few miles away; still, we trusted we were safe.

SIM's Western Africa Field missionary headquarters was separate from the ELWA compound and located nearer to the heart of the city on the main Careysburg road between the ELWA junction and the local Spriggs-Payne Airfield. President Samuel Doe's Executive Mansion lay only a couple of miles down the road. Though I occasionally had duties and recorded programs at the ELWA compound where Beth and I lived with our baby, my office was located in the SIM building downtown. A number of Americans also worked with me in the building, so I figured no harm could come to me there.

It was about four miles on foot from our house on the ELWA campus to SIM's field headquarters. I remember walking to work that morning and enjoying the warm sunshine and vibrant flowers. Though peril might be looming somewhere over the horizon, I felt at peace. I was happy to be alive, happy to be married to Beth, and happy to be a father.

I'd only been at the office for a few minutes, however, when I bumped into one of the other native Liberian missionaries. He looked at me with raised eyebrows. "Why'd you come in here today, Tony?" he asked.

"The mission," I said. "I have work to do."

"Haven't you heard?"

"Heard what? Are you talking about the rebels surrounding the city?"

"Of course."

"We've survived Doe and his reign for years now. They pretty much leave us alone. No one's going to attack SIM headquarters here or the ELWA campus with the hospital and broadcasting facility. There are too many foreign missionaries here."

"I wouldn't count on it, Tony. Not this time. Besides, things are different for us native Liberians."

"You're talking about the hatred between tribes fueled by Doe."

"Exactly. You know he blames the Gio for rising up against him. The AFL troops are going through neighborhoods and marking Gio houses. They're rounding up all of the Gio men and taking most of them out and shooting them in the head. And on the other side, Charles Taylor and the rebels aren't any better—maybe even worse. They're on the hunt for anyone of Krahn or Mandingo birth because Doe is Krahn, and many of the Mandingos are said to be helping him or acting as spies. I've heard the rebels are doing unspeakable things to Mandingos and Krahns and anyone else they suspect may have anything to do with Doe's government. Didn't you tell me your mother is Mandingo?"

"Yes."

"If the rebels come, you'd be wise to lay low and keep quiet about that. Just talk about your father's tribe. Make sure they know you're Belle. Say nothing of Mandingos."

"Of course. Thank you, brother. I understand."

The man took my arm and pulled me into a quiet corner apart from the foreigners working in the office. "Remember when we laughed about our little Soweto?"

"Yeah, I do."

"You know I love SIM and ELWA. Jesus has changed my life, and working here has been like a dream come true."

"For me, too."

"As much as I love most of these foreign missionaries, you better than anyone know they don't always understand how dangerous things can get."

"Yes. I understand."

"No matter how much they may love us, it's different for them than for us living here. None of the fighters hate them like they hate us. I've heard it's very bad, Tony. Charles Taylor's rebel soldiers especially—those doing the fighting and killing—some of them give lip service to God, but what they really believe in is black magic, the special supernatural powers of the witch doctor. He's recruited many teenage boys into his rebel force. He and his commanders have convinced most of them they are invincible and cannot be killed by bullets."

"We've been hearing rumors about such things."

"Well, they're true. I've seen some of these boys parading around in fright wigs and wearing outlandish costumes with strings of bullets strapped to their chests and big guns they barely know how to shoot. A lot of them are also on drugs given to them by their commanders. They're unpredictable, very dangerous."

Before we could even finish our conversation, the sharp staccato of gunshots erupted outside. They sounded as though coming from just down the street.

"Everybody down!" One of the SIM administrators raced down the corridor yelling. We all dove to the floor.

"What's happening?" I asked the administrator.

"Apparently some of Taylor's forces have made it into the city. We just received a warning from the American embassy."

Things were apparently changing fast.

As if on cue, the sounds of automatic weapons firing echoed through the open windows of the building. Bullets hissed through the air as rounds slammed into the plaster and concrete walls, breaking off chunks that splintered and fell to the ground. The firing was broken by intermittent periods of silence before a new series of bangs would burst forth. We all lay still on our stomachs.

"I saw some AFL soldiers going into the building across the street earlier," my friend whispered. "Looks like we may be caught in the crossfire between them and some of the rebels."

So much for the sense of security and immunity I'd felt working for the largest, most prominent foreign mission in the city. Now here we were, trapped in a strategic location the rebels had an interest in attacking.

Everyone in the building went into survival mode. For the next several hours, we lay on the floor, listening to the sporadic shooting and explosions with bullets whizzing by, talking quietly, and praying. I prayed for Beth and Abigail back at the house on the ELWA compound, pleading to God for their safety and for Jesus to give Beth strength and peace of mind. One of the administrators was still in contact with the compound, at least, and he assured us that all remained quiet there.

As the bullets flew over our heads, I also thought about Mama and what might be happening to her and the rest of my family in our village. Was she still alive? Had Balumah been attacked or Mama forced to flee? I doubted my native village was on anybody's list of strategic locations, but it was mostly Muslim; Mama wasn't the only person from the Mandingo tribe there. There was no way to know one way or the other. Everything was different in Liberia now. Communication with Balumah was impossible.

As the afternoon dragged on into early evening, the shooting gradually waned. Finally, it stopped altogether, and relative silence descended on the neighborhood around the SIM headquarters.

Had the rebels retreated? Were the AFL soldiers still in the area? We continued lying on the floor.

After what seemed forever, we heard the sound of footsteps running on the street outside. A boy no more than seven or eight years old appeared in the doorway.

"The soldiers are gone," he announced, out of breath from running, before turning to continue on to the next building.

I pushed to my feet, feeling lightheaded and nauseated but thankful to be alive. A few minutes later, another administrator appeared.

"We've got a couple of cars waiting outside," he said. "There's room for all of us. We need to get back to the ELWA compound before dark."

He didn't have to tell us twice. We hurried outside. My friend and I piled into a backseat of a van with a handful of others as a steady drizzle began to fall. Every seat was taken, and I found myself jammed against a back window watching the road as we drove away. There was no sign of the soldiers or the rebels who'd been battling around us all day. Had all of the fighters fled?

Normally on my way home from work, I'd have to contend with crowds of people either making their way home or heading out in the cool of the evening for shopping and other activities. Now it seemed we were riding through a ghost town. The streets seemed to be haunted by a sad emptiness fueled by fear. A few faces peered out at us as we passed, but most civilians were staying out of sight, keeping their heads down in advance of the approaching nightfall.

As we drove along, I could see that some of the homes and buildings along the route to the ELWA compound were now pockmarked with broken windows and bullet holes. A wave of weariness filled my soul. My thoughts ran back to the time, not too many years before, when I'd trudged along some of these same thoroughfares, bustling with people, plying my trade as a teen street vendor.

Pulling into the ELWA compound, we were greeted by a much relieved contingent of fellow staff members. Unbeknownst to me, Beth had faced her own trauma while I'd been gone, hearing about the battle from the other missionaries and listening to the sounds of gunfire and explosions in the distance—not knowing what had become of me or if I'd ever be coming back.

I ran to our house and burst through the door, shouting, "Beth? Beth, where are you?"

She appeared in the doorway to the room where Abigail slept, her face stained with tears. "You're alive!"

We collapsed into one another's arms and wept.

CHAPTER TWENTY-FOUR

Where Were You?

Inside the cramped, makeshift arrival gate at Robertson Airport, Bentley and I trudged with our backpacks through the stale air. Military generators were keeping some lights on, but that was about all. The only form of cooling came from a single rickety fan someone had propped in a corner, a stark contrast with the air-conditioned comfort of the plane.

The baggage claim area pulsed with noise as it filled wall-to-wall with hot, sweaty passengers. Still, the scene was not without some comic relief. We all watched as a lone chicken that had escaped from somewhere slowly strode across the floor and out the arrival gate toward the runway.

"Looks like somebody lost their dinner," the "Nightmare-ville" joker from the plane commented.

This time, we all chuckled. But I cut short my mirth, remembering the days when such a chicken might have meant the difference between life and death for Beth and me. Bentley and I were traveling light with just one backpack apiece. We stood in line while airport immigration personnel checked passports from behind tall desks. On the far side, I could see a large room full of tables where customs officers were performing baggage checks under the watchful eye of armed UN peacekeepers. Security was tight in this post-9/11 environment.

Beyond that, if past history was any guide, the customs personnel were not just searching for weapons and other dangers but for anything else they might be able to confiscate, or better yet, to which they might be able to assess an "import fee"—aka, a bribe. Welcome to the Republic of Liberia!

When our turn finally came, I stepped forward ahead of Bentley to the immigration desk. Since I was not yet an American citizen, I'd been able to receive an extension on my US R-1 visa in order to travel between the United States and other countries on my Liberian passport. The immigration official, an older woman, took this now and checked my face against the photo.

"Your name is Anthony Abdullah Kono Weedor?"

"Yes."

"And you are Liberian?"

"Yes."

"How long have you been gone from this country?"

"Thirteen years."

She raised an eyebrow, glancing over the immigration control paperwork I'd filled out on the plane. "Living in America? A pastor?"

"That's right."

"What is the purpose of your trip?"

"I'm here to try to see my mother."

"Mmmm. And you still have other relatives here?"

"Yes. Many."

"How long will you be here?"

"One week."

"Not thinking of staying?"

"Not this trip."

"Mmmm. Who's your companion here?" She looked behind me toward Bentley, who now stepped forward and handed her his US passport. She looked at the photo and his face, then at his paperwork. "You are a medical doctor. You live in Colorado, too?"

"Yes," he said.

"Staying one week also?"

"Yes."

She turned back to me, gesturing toward Bentley. "What is your relationship with this man?"

"We're friends and colleagues. We were in seminary together in Denver."

She jutted out her jaw, seeming impressed that I, a Liberian pastor, was claiming a prestigious North American medical professional as a friend and colleague. "Okay. Welcome back to Liberia."

Stamping both passports, she handed them back to us. "Good luck and be careful."

"Thank you. We will."

Passing through a narrow doorway, we joined another line and waited our turn for the customs inspection. Armed UN peacekeepers guarded the customs tables and exit. Bentley leaned over and whispered, "Well, that was easy enough,"

"Right," I said. "I wish it had been that easy to leave."

Out of the corner of my eye, I spotted a stocky man in uniform standing between the armed guards and the customs personnel who were checking over the luggage. He was staring at me, a clipboard in his hand. I looked away, but a few moments later I felt a tap on my shoulder. It was the clipboard man.

He glanced from me to Bentley, then asked me to step to the side and place my bag on a separate table. Offering Bentley a look of resignation, I stepped out of line and followed the man to a table where he proceeded to take control of my backpack. He was the chief official, he informed me. Apparently, I was being singled out for particular scrutiny—but that wasn't all. The man kept looking toward Bentley. I realized he had an additional agenda: he was trying to use me to draw my white traveling companion into an uncomfortable confrontation to extract a bribe. Bentley started to move toward us, but I motioned him away and turned to face the official. Whatever happened, I decided, was going to stay between us Liberians.

Undoing the clasps on my pack, the assessor started pulling clothes and other items out, looking over the contents. He also asked more questions. Where did I live in America? How long had I been there? What church was I a part of?

I answered as politely as I could, knowing this man had the power to cause me any amount of trouble. I wasn't sure what exactly he was after with his probing, but whatever it was, he wasn't finding my answers satisfactory; clearly I'd angered him by intervening with Bentley.

"Where were you?" he asked, his voice suddenly rising so others around us could hear too.

"I beg your pardon?"

"I said, *where were you?*"

"What do you mean?" I was genuinely puzzled.

His expression hardened into a coldness that reminded me of the darkest side of my culture. His eyes burned like empty coals. "Where have you been while Liberia has suffered? Where have you been while we here have been eating hungry rice?"

Hungry rice was the common name for *fonio*, an African variety of millet. Ironically, in the West it was now actually being touted as an imported health food, but in Liberia it was what the poorest of the poor were lucky to have available; hungry rice had become synonymous with starvation.

I'd dealt with this type of official before: a professional bully, who'd been bequeathed a limited amount of official authority that he was intent on using to try to control others. He was someone for whom fear was only to be pushed away and never acknowledged, let alone dealt with, someone for whom anger became a driving force, a tool to grind down everyone around him. Sensing some sort of a confrontation, a small group of people had begun to gather around us, many of them native Liberians. The chief assessor glared at me, awaiting my answer.

"Running from people like you," I said without raising my voice.

His eyes narrowed and a vein in his neck began to bulge. He started making threats, but a woman in the crowd who'd overhead us rose to my defense.

"That's right," she said, matching the assessor's tone so everyone else around us could hear. "We've all been running from people like you."

A few others joined in, arguing back and forth with one another. The big man stalked toward the woman, and I stepped in between, thinking this was not the way things were supposed to go upon my return to Liberia. I could only imagine what Bentley might be thinking.

But just when things were threatening to escalate out of control, a peacekeeping soldier, who'd been standing quietly to one side, sauntered into the middle of the crowd. He repositioned his hand over the trigger guard of the submachine gun slung over his shoulder. He didn't say anything because he didn't need to. His presence quieted everyone. Even the angry customs assessor seemed to get the message, at least on the surface.

"Eh, bah, he knows book," one of the other officials called out from across the room, referring to me and my apparent education and waving his hand as if I wasn't worth the trouble. "Let the book man in."

And that seemed to be that. The assessor closed my backpack, and the crowd began to disperse.

The man slid the pack across the table back toward me. "Just tell me one thing, Reverend," he said in a low voice so no one else could hear. "Why are you coming back here now?"

I ignored him, shouldered my bag, and turned and walked away. He reminded me in some ways of my long dead father, much easier to be angry than face one's deepest fears.

CHAPTER TWENTY-FIVE

Not Anymore

In July 1990, soon after the gun battle around the SIM head-quarters downtown, our ELWA compound began taking in refugees from the fighting. They came in small groups at first, showing up at the gate and asking for a safe place to stay. Then they started coming by the dozens. Before too long, they started showing up by the hundreds as word spread among the civilian population in and around Monrovia that ELWA was a place they might escape from invading rebel forces as well as the brutal reach of Doe's soldiers.

By mid-July, six months after Charles Taylor and his ragtag rebel army had invaded Liberia and begun fighting their way toward the capital, our campus had become home to more than twenty thousand Liberians seeking refuge from the bullets. They camped in makeshift tents and shelters everywhere the eye could see. The beautiful palm trees lining the beach were stripped of their fronds to be used as roofing, makeshift containers, and disposable plates.

The campus administrators were able to maintain a certain semblance of order. But sanitation soon became a problem, and the smell of human waste was carried throughout the compound by the ocean breezes. Many of the foreign missionaries had been evacuated back to their own countries by this point, and hundreds of luckier refugees crammed into those homes standing empty. With growing violence outside the gates, national SIM staff had been moved inside the ELWA compound gates, so Beth and I and baby Abigail were now relocated from our lodgings across the road to the home of an expat missionary family who'd already been evacuated. We took in a number of refugees as well while even more camped out on our porch.

As the month of July wore on, word spread throughout the compound about heavier fighting in Monrovia. Some said that Charles Taylor's NPFL rebels had already taken most of the city but respected ELWA's long history of service to Liberia enough to leave the compound in peace. By now, this included national ELWA staff and a number of remaining expatriate missionaries as well as thousands of other citizens sheltering within our grounds.

Others, perhaps better informed, claimed the NPFL rebels were no respecters of persons and would be intent on seizing our radio station and powerful broadcast towers to further their growing control of the country and transmit their messages throughout the country. A number of expat missionaries told us that their various embassies had advised them to be ready to evacuate. Despite such warnings, they didn't want to abandon us and their other native colleagues. Unlike the expat missionaries, we were not under the protection of any outside government. If the fighting descended upon us, where could we go?

On July 22, with resistance from Doe's army having melted away, Taylor's rebels finally entered the ELWA compound. These "soldiers" were mostly boys armed with AK-47s and handguns, which they would fire off into the air every few minutes to intimidate the cowering civilians. They had no uniforms, but wore filthy shorts or jeans. They were either bare-chested or clad in ragged T-shirts with ropes tied around their heads as voodoo talismans.

Some even wore strange outfits—women's wigs, choir gowns, or skirts—as if they'd jumped straight out of some B-grade horror movie. Despite the bizarre scene, many among the crowd of civilians began to cheer for their "liberators," perhaps in hopes of currying favor with those now in control. The rebels laughed and fired their guns in the air again and again.

But any hopes that the rebel victory would restore peace quickly faded. Charles Taylor and his commanders proved relentless in their hatred and pursuit of those they deemed traitorous among native Liberians, in particular Krahns and Mandingos or anyone with ties to the Doe government. They began mounting house-to-house searches, separating out men with the wrong tribal heritage, whether or not they'd actually fought for the Doe regime. These they'd march away at gunpoint, many never to be seen again.

On the morning of July 25th, Beth and I ate a meager breakfast, then went out to share some of our food with others who'd taken refuge in and around our home. I wanted to go across the campus to the radio station, but due to the danger of the situation, Beth had begged me to stay home, so I did.

Toward midday, all was quiet in the back of the house where I sat reading my Bible. Since dawn, we'd been hearing sporadic gunfire but were unsure what to make of the situation. In the kitchen, Beth was preparing our noon meal, with Abigail sleeping next to her in her basket, when a glance out the window left her frozen with fear.

"Tony!"

I knew from the tone of Beth's voice that something was wrong. Hurrying toward the front of the house, I caught a glimpse through the window of what had caused her to cry out. A group of young men still barely into their teens were advancing on our small house. They strode onto our porch and banged on the door.

"Open the door and come out!" one of them shouted. "Everybody get outside!"

Beth snatched Abigail from her basket. I could see the fear in her eyes. I motioned for her to take Abigail to the safety of our bedroom. "Let me talk to them."

The teen "soldiers" pounded on the door, and as I saw Beth and Abigail retreat from sight, I went to the door and opened it. Before me stood our invading army—four boys somewhere between thirteen and fifteen years old dressed in blue jeans and dirty T-shirts and shouldering AK-47s.

One of the oldest stepped forward, clearly the leader. A bandana covered his head, and a cigarette dangled from his mouth. His bloodshot eyes were blank as though high on some drug. "This your house, my man?"

"It is," I said. I could hear Abigail wailing and Beth trying to soothe her somewhere behind me.

"Not anymore, my man. You all need to get out of this house. It belongs to us now."

I knew better than to argue. It looked like we were going to be forced to walk away with little more than the clothes on our backs. Beth emerged from the back of the house, Abigail already strapped to her back in a carrying shawl. Stepping forward, she pleaded bravely with the teens to let her get some things for the baby. They allowed her to do this, but I was kept on the porch with their guns pointed at me.

When Beth came out, they insisted on searching through the few belongings she'd gathered and made sure neither of us were carrying any weapons. Then they ordered us to leave the compound and cross the battle lines to NPFL-controlled territory where they were gathering many other native Liberians. We could either comply or be marched off and shot.

We didn't try to resist since we knew others had already been killed by machete or beheaded. Sadly, we walked down the road toward the compound gate. It was the last time we would ever see that house.

Beth had taken advantage of her few moments in the house. In addition to supplies for the baby and a few personal items, she'd also managed to stuff some of my preaching clothes into a knapsack along with my Bible and the collection of Francis Schaeffer books I so treasured. Her act of unselfish, extravagant love for me in the face of such danger caused me to nearly break down and cry.

We would carry that Bible and those books with us throughout whatever danger or horror that came next. They provided no physical protection or practical benefit like the food or water we could have taken instead. In point of fact, they weighed us down. Not once did I consider abandoning them, however; to us they offered a hope no AK-47, rocket-propelled grenade, or murdering rebels would ever be able to overcome.

CHAPTER TWENTY-SIX

Parade Rest

The 2004 UN peacekeeping mission to Liberia consisted of soldiers from a number of different countries. The Nigerian officer in charge at the airport looked relaxed as he stood inside the terminal entrance surveying the arriving passengers. His salt-and-pepper mustache complemented his dark skin. His green camouflage uniform and wire frame glasses gave him an air of authority.

Having watched from a distance the tense exchange between me and the customs official, he stood at parade rest and nodded at Bentley and me with a bemused expression as we exited the terminal.

"What was that all about back there?" Bentley asked, looking back over his shoulder at the terminal where the official was now talking to other passengers.

"I guess the damage here goes even deeper than I thought," I said.

Outside, the Liberian night washed over us, rich with humidity and the familiar florid smells of my childhood.

A pair of UN tanks was positioned in front of the airport entrance alongside a line of trucks armed with heavy machine guns and a squad of soldiers. Control of the country's only working major airport had apparently been a vital prize in the heavy fighting these soldiers had been brought in to end.

There were no buses or taxis or any other sign of public transportation. Just beyond the UN security perimeter, I noticed a faded Toyota Land Cruiser waiting among a throng of private vehicles crowding the pickup area. From behind the wheel, a small man was smiling and waving to us. Though I hadn't seen him in years, I recognized him instantly.

"There's our ride," I told Bentley.

Wankollie was a longtime SIM staff worker who, along with others, had somehow managed to keep the ELWA radio station on the air. I'd been told most of the compound buildings and infrastructure had been ransacked or destroyed in the fighting, but thanks to the work of men like Wankollie, ELWA had only ceased broadcasting for an eighteen-month period during the worst of the fighting.

Brother Wankollie leapt from the vehicle as we approached. He smiled broadly as he reached out to embrace me. "Look at you, Tony. I cannot believe you are here."

"Thank you for coming to pick us up. I know it must not have been easy."

"You're right, my friend, nothing is easy here anymore." His Liberian accent rang comfortably in my ears. My own had become somewhat Americanized during my studies in the United States. "The SIM office told me about your plans to try to reunite with your mother. It's good you're here."

He turned toward Bentley. "And this must be your friend, the medical doctor."

"Yes." I introduced the two of them. "Bentley and I went to seminary together."

Wankollie smiled warmly as the two men shook hands. "Welcome to our country."

Bentley is one of the most warm-spirited, kindly men I have ever met, at ease with any stranger, and I was glad to see an immediate liking between my two friends. Wankollie motioned us toward his vehicle.

"Come. We must get going. It's only forty kilometers to the ELWA compound, but the UN soldiers patrol the road heavily at night, and there will be checkpoints looking for weapons. It will be slow going."

CHAPTER TWENTY-SEVEN

Twisted Exodus

For the thousands who'd taken shelter at the ELWA compound that summer of 1990, the day of reckoning had finally come.

A stampede ensued as we were all forced to leave the campus. There was little direction from our so-called "liberators" except to tell us to start walking in the direction of rebel-held territory. As a fellow Christian missionary later described, we had all become unwilling participants in some twisted, hallucinogenic approximation of the biblical exodus.

Once through the compound gate, the massive crowd splintered into pieces. Some groups broke into a run for what they hoped would be the safety of the bush. We moved with guarded steps, hoping to not draw attention to ourselves. All around us, rebels continued to fire their weapons into the air. Men they deemed suspicious for whatever reason were hauled away from their loved ones to be questioned or killed.

Beth and I soon found ourselves walking with a small group of friends along Duport Road, which led from the ELWA junction in the direction of the public radio station. We'd barely cleared the area when a fresh battle erupted, raining bursts of automatic weapon fire to either side of us. The shooting came from remaining elements of Doe's army, and we realized were in the middle of a counterattack being mounted against the rebels.

Caught in the crossfire, people fled in all directions. To one side of me, a young man shot in the face fell dead. Tracer rounds zipped through the air. A grenade exploded not far behind us. Our small group somehow made it to the relative safety of some trees, but we had to keep moving. To this day, I have no words to adequately describe the horrors of everything I saw and felt in those terrible hours. Had I only known the worst was yet to come.

***

Doe's soldiers were soon driven back, leaving our "liberators" free to continue their reign of chaos and horror. Some time later, those of us who remained in the crowd were herded toward a large open area bounded by fields.

By this time, some of Taylor's drug-crazed teen soldiers were randomly selecting certain victims to terrorize for sport, forcing them to squirm along on their stomachs toward a line of trees. Their victims were told this would earn them a chance at being "set free." Instead, the teens took pot shots at the crawlers with their AK-47s, wounding or killing them to the laughter and catcalls of the other rebels.

As Beth and I and the rest of our party were herded toward a rebel checkpoint, we did our best to blend in among the bedraggled crowd of several hundred men, women, and children of all ages. Abigail screamed in hunger as she rode on

Beth's back, but we didn't dare slow down for Beth to try to nurse her. I moved alongside Beth to hold Abigail's tiny hand, and she calmed down, at least for the time being.

"Tony," Beth said under her breath. "Are you still carrying your SIM employee card?"

"Yes, I think so. What about it?"

"The rebels are searching out Mandingos and anyone who might be with Doe. If they see the word Muslim on your employee card, they might just think you're Mandingo and kill you."

She was right. My SIM picture ID identified me by my employee title as Director of Muslim Outreach for West Africa. We knew the rebels along with Doe's Krahns were hunting Mandingo Muslims. Most of the rebels were barely literate, so trying to explain that "Muslim Outreach" on my card didn't make me a Muslim might get us killed.

A long line had formed at the checkpoint. We were still some distance from the front, but we would have to pass through soon enough. Beth whispered, "I have an idea. If you can take out your card without anyone seeing, you can slip it down my back under Abigail's blanket. No one will be searching the baby."

Without another word, praying no one saw me, I did as Beth suggested, and we continued to move up in the line. When our turn came to pass through the checkpoint, I held my breath while the rebel soldiers questioned Beth, paying no attention to Abigail, who had thankfully fallen asleep on Beth's back.

Then it was my turn. When the rebel soldier in charge asked for my identification, I simply showed him my driver's license, which said nothing about my job with the mission. The rebel eyed me with suspicion. "Krahn?"

"No," I said. "Belle."

He continued staring at me while Beth and Abigail waited anxiously just beyond the checkpoint. Then he turned and whispered to one of the rebel teens standing next to him. The teen looked over at me and in the Belle language casually asked how I was feeling. When I replied in fluent Belle, the boy nodded at his commander, and the man in charge waved me through.

Others weren't so lucky. We saw two men being dragged off for "questioning" and an older child being separated from her mother. We felt powerless and hopeless. We'd all heard stories about what the rebels would do if they discovered a Krahn woman who was pregnant. The woman would be murdered, her unborn child ripped from her womb and slaughtered. What kind of God, I had to wonder, could allow such brutality?

The same kind of God, I reminded myself, who'd allowed his own son to be condemned by sinful humans. The same kind of God who'd come to earth in the person of Jesus Christ and allowed himself to die a brutal death on a Roman cross.

As night fell, the shooting began again in earnest. Blasts from automatic weapons and heavy artillery were lighting up the dark sky, and random bullets were striking people in the crowd, but the rebels kept herding all of us forward. There was no time to stop, no time to think about the terror; we became walking breathing shadows who either kept moving or died.

CHAPTER TWENTY-EIGHT

The Living Lost

Wankollie helped us load our backpacks into the Land Cruiser, we climbed in, and soon we'd left the airport behind. Convoying behind another private car, a jeep full of soldiers, and a big UN supply truck, we were forced to crawl along to avoid obstacles littering the highway and enormous potholes. Fog had begun to envelope the jungle and the road. Every now and then, we came upon someone walking along the road in the darkness or a few shadows of houses, but other than these few signs of life, the glare of our headlights might as well have been moving through an empty land.

"You gentlemen must be tired," Wankollie spoke up.

"Overwhelmed is more like it," I responded. "I didn't expect conditions here to be so bad."

"People are scared." Wankollie's voice in the darkness reflected a deep sadness and resignation. "Everything has changed since you were here, Tony. We have to run the radio station completely by generator. There is no running water either. No sanitation and still only so much food. Few move around at night. It's dangerous the deeper you travel into the interior, but here, too, until we get closer to the city. That's why I'm keeping that jeep with the soldiers in sight."

"What about the ELWA guesthouse where we will be staying?"

"You will be safe there. The exterior is still standing. Unfortunately the interior has been gutted. There are no windows or doors, but at least you'll have a roof over your heads."

"That will be more than enough, thank you."

"You're very welcome. I understand from the SIM office that you are living in the United States now."

"Yes."

"Things must be different there after 9/11 and now the war in Iraq and the attack on Madrid."

"Yes. Very different. People worry about terrorism."

"Everyone here is asking if America can't protect itself, what hope is there for little Liberia? We get our only news these days through the BBC and the UN, and a little from the government station in Monrovia. Not like the old days when ELWA had our own local correspondents and news sources throughout the country so we could provide accurate reporting."

"I've been wondering how you've managed to stay on the air with so few resources."

"We just take it one step at a time," Wankollie said. "Some days, we have trouble with power and may be off the air for a little while, but we've been able to manage."

"That takes a lot of dedication!" Bentley chimed in.

Wankollie slowed to ease through a pothole. "Yes. ELWA is still bringing the gospel to West Africa. The mission hasn't changed. And if we can no longer provide much news reporting from around Liberia, we have another more personal mission these days at the station. We receive from the UN lists of people trying to find out about lost loved ones. They might be children without family or parents looking for children or people searching for relatives who've gone missing or maybe died. Every day we broadcast these messages and the names of the living lost. ELWA has become a resource for people looking to reconnect with others here in Liberia. Not just a resource, but a source of hope amidst all the fear and violence."

"The living lost," I said, feeling the weight and sadness of his words settle into my soul. "I guess I've come to the right place then to try to see my mother again."

"Yes." Wankollie's expression was unreadable in the meager reflection of the Land Cruiser's headlights. "You know, for many people outside ELWA, it could be your name on that list, Tony. Many still ask about you from time to time and wonder what happened to you. We've been able to receive word through SIM for years about you and your ministry, of course, but you know how people talk. We've tried to explain, but some don't believe you're actually alive. They think you may be a ghost."

"No ghost." The thought brought a smile to my face. "Here I am in the flesh."

"Yes," Wankollie chuckled. "And I've laid hands on you myself, so next time I'll be able to refute them."

We reached the first UN checkpoint, a barricade formed by a pair of armored cars blocking the road and manned by half a dozen soldiers. After the vehicles ahead of us were waved on through, Wankollie pulled the Land Cruiser up to the barricade and rolled down his window.

"Traveling from the airport?" one of the soldiers asked.

"Yes."

The soldier looked warily at Bentley and me while another soldier circled around the vehicle from the other side to check us out. They asked to see all of our IDs and made Wankollie get out and open the back of the Land Cruiser for inspection before finally waving us through. It took a while before we caught up again with the jeep. By this time, I had caught sight of some fires burning in the jungle and along the road.

"What's all the burning for?" I asked.

Wankollie shrugged. "Hard to know. Day and night, people are burning many things these days. Garbage. Pieces of buildings. Dead bodies. You'll be smelling smoke practically the whole time you're here."

He glanced over at me. "I wanted to ask with you living in America now. Being a former Muslim, you must get a lot of questions these days about Islam and the Americans' war on terror."

"I do. A great number of questions."

"Fear comes in many flavors, I guess," he said thoughtfully.

"Yes, it does."

We'd passed through four more UN checkpoints over the next hour when I suddenly recognized a large mangrove tree along the road. Wankollie nodded at it. "Bring back any memories?"

"Yes," I said, realizing we were nearing the ELWA compound. But my excited recognition turned to shock as the Land Cruiser drove through what remained of the compound's gate.

The ELWA campus stretched along the Liberian coast for three-quarters of a mile, its beach protected by a rocky reef that made it safe and enjoyable for swimming. I used to walk along the soft white sand of that beach at night with Beth during our ELWA days. After dark, you could see the glowing lights of downtown Monrovia shimmering across the water twelve miles away.

But looking out past the palms to the water tonight, all I could see was inky darkness. The chain link perimeter fence had been torn down, and the sign at the entrance was badly battered and scarred. Cinderblocks and other debris littered the roadway as we jolted up what had once been a well-tended gravel track. Our headlights bounced off a few remaining buildings. All were damaged and appeared unlit.

Across the compound, only a couple of dim lights battled with the night. With so little illumination, the spindly broadcast antennas were completely invisible. Like the war-battered airport terminal, what had once been a vibrant and flourishing beacon for West Africa was now swallowed up by the surrounding darkness, reduced to running on fumes.

Wankollie stopped the vehicle and cut the engine. "Welcome home."

It didn't look like the home I remembered. But as we climbed out of the Land Cruiser, I caught amidst the acrid scent of smoke from those fires we'd glimpsed earlier a familiar whiff of a salty ocean breeze and the rhythmic music of waves crashing on the beach. Other night sounds murmured from the remaining trees—tree frogs and the twitter of birds settling down to sleep. These at least hadn't changed.

Wankollie dug a fluorescent lantern from the vehicle and by its narrow beam led us toward the black hulk of a small building, the glow from his lantern cutting through the thick humidity and fluttering insects. Our destination was the ELWA guesthouse, which I remembered as a picturesque beach cottage with a corrugated tin roof that sat among a number of beachfront homes housing the expatriate missionary staff.

Shaded by palms and bright with tropical flowers climbing the walls on lattice-style trellises, the ELWA guesthouse had served as a community meeting house and host to all sorts of events from cookouts to weddings to funerals. The building's chief function was to host visiting dignitaries, pastors, foreign missionary leaders, and even African heads of state. Back then, Liberia had been the Christian jewel of West Africa and the ELWA guesthouse one of its facets.

I wished I could pass the memory of those days on to Bentley because the gray silhouette of the structure we were approaching made it hard to imagine there had ever been such a place. Only the husk of the guesthouse remained, like the outside of some hollowed-out tomb. There was no glass in the windows, and the door hung open on broken hinges. The roof remained but also looked in disrepair.

"I'm sorry there is no light here in the guesthouse," Wankollie said as we stepped inside the open doorway. "The generator power must be reserved to run the broadcast studio and towers."

There were no furnishings inside or plumbing fixtures or running water. But the floors were swept clean, whether in anticipation of our arrival or for other visitors who'd stayed here. Bentley looked around with an untroubled smile. "No problem. It'll be like camping."

Wankollie switched on another fluorescent lantern he'd brought in from the Land Cruiser. "At least you'll have a roof over your heads, and I can leave you a couple of lanterns. You should be safe here. We have a guard that patrols the campus, and you already saw the UN soldiers patrolling the road."

In our backpacks, we'd brought light sleeping bags and other necessary gear. We found bottled water and a few packaged goods provided for us in the guesthouse's dilapidated kitchen. I had also brought a battery-operated radio rechargeable by a hand crank that was a reminder of my teen years working as a vendor on Monrovia's streets and the tiny crank-powered transistor radio I'd carried back then.

After Wankollie bid us goodbye, we spread out our sleeping bags on the floor. Tucking his mosquito netting around his bedding, Bentley calmly smiled. "Well, we're a long way from Colorado," he said.

"You can say that again." I chuckled as I nearly collapsed into my bedding.

Lying beneath my mosquito net, I listened to the familiar sound of the ocean surf pounding the beach outside. I might have expected memories—good and bad—would keep me awake, but it had been a long, exhausting journey. Soon I fell fast sleep.

CHAPTER TWENTY-NINE

Not Completely Alone

In my dreams, I was back in 1990 being herded again at gunpoint through the darkness on the road toward rebel-held territory.

Sometime approaching midnight, the gunfire and explosions around us finally came to an end. It seemed even the combatants needed some sort of a break from the madness of it all.

We heard the sound of flowing water, and soon we were standing on the bank of a fast-running stream. I knew this creek well. On the far side lay Soul Clinic Mission, a humanitarian facility run by a native Liberian and his African-American wife. We could see the lights of the clinic across the water, but the stream here was chest-deep and too dangerous to try to cross in the dark. We were also told the rebels had set up a checkpoint for all those entering the clinic. Our captors ordered us all to stop along the creek bank for the night and wait our turn in the morning. We were only allowed to approach the water to drink.

Hungry and exhausted, we settled down among the crowd, too traumatized to speak.

Then, in one of the strangest sights I'd ever witnessed, the rebels began to sing. The songs they chose were patriotic Liberian songs, and they forced us at gunpoint to sing along with them. I found it hard to imagine anything patriotic about our situation, but perhaps these deluded young men needed to convince themselves that their random killing of innocent people served some higher purpose.

After a while, the singing tapered off; the rebels seemed to run out of songs. Their songs meant for inspiration and unity had instead withered into false messages with no substance. They were musical ghosts. Beth and I huddled together with our small group of friends, praying but fearing the worst.

There was good reason to be afraid. After an hour of waiting, a group of barefoot, shirtless rebels waded into our group and jerked me to my feet along with several other men.

"Let's go. Now!" they shouted.

One of them prodded me with the barrel of his gun. Rising to my feet, I turned to glance at Beth and Abigail in the dark, wondering if these might be the last memories I would ever have of them. Beth muffled sobs with the other women as more and more men were separated from their loved ones. The women knew any protest would only make things worse for the men.

I obeyed the urging of the gun barrel in my back and walked forward with the others. Though it was hard to see in the dark, the rebels kept pushing us down a trail we could feel with our feet. On and on we walked, farther and farther away from our families.

After what seemed a long time, we stumbled into an open field. The grass here was tall, making it more difficult to move. Still, the rebels herded us forward, and now we had to worry about stepping on a scorpion or deadly black mamba snake hidden in the grass.

The rebels ordered us to stop and sit down on the ground. Not far away, I could see the dark silhouette of other groups of men. What did these young fighters want with us? Would we be drugged and conscripted to fight in Taylor's army along with them?

I worried about what might be happening to Beth and our precious baby daughter. Just when it seemed things couldn't get any worse, a clap of thunder roared from overhead and a heavy rain began to pound the ground. The sky opened up on us as only a monsoon storm can, instantly drenching us to the bone.

I looked around, hoping that in the brief confusion sowed by the storm there might be some opportunity for escape, but without any warning, shots boomed forth and piercing staccato rounds from the rebels' automatic weapons raked the ground. Shouts and screams rose above the rain as some tried to run, but everywhere it seemed the dying slumped or fell to the ground. The two men nearest me had already been shot through the head, and as more and more shots rang out, I decided my only hope was to play dead, so I slumped to the side and collapsed with my face in the mud.

Closing my eyes, I lay perfectly still and willed myself to barely breathe. The shots finally stopped; there were no more shouts and screams.

The only sound came from the rain pounding the jungle, which suddenly seemed to intensify. Had the rebels gone?

Had they left us all for dead? Maybe they were still watching from a distance for any signs of life. I wasn't about to move or open my eyes to find out.

As the minutes turned into hours, I could do nothing but lie still, my head turned to one side to keep my nostrils above the mud and water. With my clothing soaked through and the rain continuing to pound my prone body, I was now chilled and shivering badly. At least I felt no pain, so I was pretty sure I hadn't been shot. Whispering a prayer for my family and for all those caught up in the violence, I finally drifted off to sleep.

***

Awakening from a nightmare of flying bodies, I opened my eyes to the brightening glimmer of dawn. The rain had stopped, and I caught a patch of blue sky in my peripheral vision. Shivering wet and cold, I was still afraid to move.

I strained to hear any noise from the rebels but heard nothing beyond the normal bird calls and insect whines of a jungle morning. Finally, I gathered the courage to raise my head. Looking around, I discovered I was completely alone.

No, not completely alone. I rose to my feet and looked around. The two men who'd fallen beside me during the shooting the night before lay dead nearby. A little farther away, the corpses of the men who'd marched into the field with me littered the deep grass.

Why hadn't I been killed? Had God sent the drenching rain to save me? Had others managed to escape? There was no time to dwell on such questions. All that mattered was that the rebels were gone for now. I set out in search of Beth and Abigail.

Backtracking along the trail to where I'd left them the night before, I found them among other women and children curled up asleep. Not wanting to awaken the baby, I squatted beside my wife and gently touched her shoulder.

"Hello, Beth." I whispered. "Are you okay?"

Her eyes flew open. She cried out and punched me in the arm for giving her such a fright before flinging her arms around me as we collapsed together in tears of relief. I don't know if Beth has ever completely forgiven me for such a casual greeting after our night of terror in the bush.

"I kept saying to myself they might as well kill me early," she told me later. "If you died, they might as well kill me, too."

***

We finally made it across the stream to Soul Clinic but only stayed there for a couple of nights. With the fighting and random killings continuing all around us, it was too dangerous to remain. Besides, we had little food and no water except the stream. Leaving the clinic grounds, we joined the stream of civilians fleeing in the direction of the University of Liberia's Fendell Campus, where we'd heard better refuge might be found.

A few hours later, at a checkpoint on the road to the campus, the leader of a ragtag group of soldiers pointed at me. "You!"

With the barrel of his gun, he motioned for me to move apart from Beth and Abigail. Yet again, I was questioned about my tribal ethnicity. Was I Mandingo? Was I Krahn?

By now, we'd heard from other refugees even more horror stories about how Krahns and Mandingos were being systematically purged. Along with the slaughter of pregnant women, their babies brutally cut out of their wombs, some Krahn and Mandingo women had been forced to watch their husbands being savagely butchered before they themselves were raped.

"I am Belle," I told the rebel leader, a youth no more than sixteen or seventeen years old. Again, I added a few phrases in the Belle dialect.

He glared at me for a long moment. Then he snorted in disgust and directed me to move back into line in front of Beth.

Moments later, she whispered over my shoulder. "We can't stay on the road."

"I know."

A half a mile down the highway, just before the cutoff for the international airport, we heard bursts of gunfire and screaming from somewhere up ahead. We started running toward the trees, with Beth still carrying Abigail on her back, hoping to melt into the bush and get away.

CHAPTER THIRTY

Shadow Walls

A decade and a half later, in the remains of the ELWA guest-house, I opened my eyes to the rhythmic crash of the surf outside and bright sunlight angling through the glassless window openings.

Insects buzzed through the room; I was glad I'd slept under the mosquito netting. For a moment, Liberia felt like a long-lost friend. I'd almost forgotten its natural beauty. The rivers flowing into the sea. The gentle cooling of the rain. The wind in the rainforest canopy sounding like the *shhhhh* of a water-fall pouring over a high face of rock. But then I remembered the shattered remains of the country we'd flown into the night before, a land overrun by fear.

"Are you awake?" Bentley's voice interrupted my reverie. I turned my head to see him sitting on his sleeping bag with his back to the wall, thumbing through a small paperback Bible.

"Barely." I pulled the mosquito netting away and wriggled out of my sleeping bag. Standing up, I shook them both out.

Wankollie's face appeared in the open doorway. "Good morning, gentlemen. I hope you slept well."

"Better than I expected," I told him. "I don't think I stirred all night. How about you, Bentley?"

Bentley had risen to his feet too. He smiled warmly at Wankollie. "Not quite as good as the Hilton, but I suppose it will have to do."

Wankollie laughed. "Good. You two had a long trip. Brother Tony, your sister Victoria called the radio station this morning. Apparently, some of your family knows you're here?"

"Yes. I sent word through an uncle."

"Good. Your sister says to tell you she is coming here tomorrow to see you and bring you news about your mother and the rest of your family. Meanwhile, how about if we head over to my house for some breakfast? Then maybe you'd like to stop in at the studio. Nothing like you'd remember, Tony, but at least you can see how we're back in business now."

"I'd like that. Thank you," I said.

Bentley and I followed Wankollie to his house, where we enjoyed a typical Liberian breakfast of sweet calla cakes along with sliced pineapple and mango, all washed down with instant coffee. Then we accompanied him to the ELWA radio studio.

Seeing the small, squat building sitting in front of a grove of palm trees with its windows facing the road brought back many memories, but inside nothing was the same. The original equipment had all been looted and replaced by somewhat newer, if still dated, donated studio furnishings. They were on the air, and a man I didn't recognize was behind the mike. Tears began to well up in my eyes at the heroism of these individuals who continued broadcasting the word about Jesus with so little.

Compassion showed through Wankollie's eyes. "I know it's not the same, brother. The soldiers and the rebels all had their turn at looting here. But God is good. And since the UN came, things are slowly getting better, though it may never be the same as before. Too much killing, I'm afraid."

"Too much fear," I added. He nodded.

It occurred to me then that the biggest export in the world at this time in history wasn't grain or oil or any physical product; it was fear. Islamic terrorism, in particular, exported fear from one culture to another, almost anywhere you looked on the globe. I thought of Mama living somewhere in a slum only a few miles away from where we were standing. How had she and the rest of my family survived all these years? What kind of starvation and trauma had they been forced to endure? Had Mama been told I was back?

Wankollie steered us out of the radio station. "We'll come back later so you can greet the other ELWA staff who used to work here with you. They all want to welcome you back, the new ones as well."

Later that morning, Bentley and I walked across the road to look around the area where Beth and I used to live. A truckload of UN soldiers whizzed by followed by a Nigerian armored vehicle with its whip antennae and imposing gun turret. Everywhere we looked, the devastation was made starker by the light of day. Burned out cars. Deserted homes. The skeletal remains of buildings.

The smell of smoke and cooking mingled with the stench of human waste. A few people peered out at us from within what was left of their dwellings but just as quickly they disappeared from sight. You could feel their fear. Although it had been a number of months since the UN peacekeepers imposed a ceasefire, bands of armed teenagers—leftover remnants of Charles Taylor's army who apparently had yet to accept the new reality—still roamed the area after dark, and strong-arm robberies and assaults weren't uncommon.

I started to recognize familiar landmarks from the peaceful years we'd lived here, and from that terrible day when the rebels had driven us out. The brick wall where one of my fellow ELWA missionaries had been shot dead. The broken pipes protruding from the ground that used to connect to the area's water system.

I paused for a moment to stare down at the broken pipes. Bentley asked me if I was all right. I told him I was, but that wasn't entirely true. For some reason, the sight of that brick wall and the pipes made me think of historical photos I'd seen of Hiroshima, the first time in history a nuclear weapon was used against a civilian population. Haunting shadows of incinerated human beings were still immortalized there on some of the Japanese city's walls.

In a way, the ELWA campus in Liberia had become my personal Hiroshima, I realized—less well known to history perhaps, but just as devastating to me.

CHAPTER THIRTY-ONE

Heads

Neither Beth nor I slept much that sweltering 1990 night after making our escape from the road. By the next morning, we'd been running and hiding for hours and were both so thirsty we no longer even felt our hunger. Beth looked exhausted, but she refused to let me take Abigail from her back. I knew she was right. If the rebels spotted us, they would shoot at me first because I was a man. If I were carrying Abigail, she might be killed too.

Pressing forward, we finally came to the banks of another sizable creek. It was quiet here, the sound of gunfire long faded into the distance. The swift-moving current promised blessed relief for our thirst, and I felt the fear and tension drain from my shoulders as I lowered the knapsack to reach for our empty water bottle.

Then a rounded object approached around a bend upstream. I assumed it was just some kind of debris and paid little attention until two similar objects appeared followed by many more. That was when I realized they were human heads. The heads were attached to bodies, butting and banging against each other like macabre bumper cars jostling for position in a horror show race.

Beth and I clung to one another in revulsion as the corpses bobbed past us.

"What do you want to do?" she asked.

"I don't know," I said.

On Beth's back, Abigail screamed in hunger and thirst, and Beth turned toward me with tears streaming down her face.

"We have to drink, Tony. We have to drink the water and give some to Abigail or we'll die."

She was right. What choice did we have?

CHAPTER THIRTY-TWO

Broken Mirror

As soon as Bentley and I returned to the ELWA guesthouse, I tuned the solar-powered radio I'd brought to the ELWA station. The "lost loved ones" broadcast was going on, and I listened to the litany of missing people for whom relatives were searching. There was a David Joseph and his wife and family. A Pastor Samuel James. A woman looking for her mother. Two wives looking for information about their missing husbands.

Several children had also been found. The radio announcer gave their names and approximate ages—Eleanor, age seven, Albert, age six, Teka, Akeela, William, Abraham Jabbie. And on and on.

I didn't recognize any of the names. As I listened, I stared out through the damaged doorway toward the beach where waves were crashing on the sand. The surf was rough today. I tried to imagine myself in the shoes of the people who'd called into the radio station searching for their loved ones. I looked over at Bentley, who was listening as well.

"So many," he said, looking sad.

"Yes."

"You think most of them are dead?"

"Maybe. Probably."

After lunch, another driver from ELWA took us into the city to have a look around. We passed a field where piles of canvas bags stuffed with rice and cases of bottled water lay in front of a row of parked UN trucks. Civilians had formed a long line and were moving meekly forward in the hot sun. In contrast, the relief workers handing out food and water were congregated beneath the canvas roofing of the truck beds, the only available shade. Blue-helmeted UN soldiers watched over the distribution. They looked wary of the crowd. One of them who wore a red beret and appeared to be in command was shouting angrily at the people in line. He seemed ready to pull the trigger on the submachine slung over his shoulder at any moment.

I remembered my own time in a UN refugee camp, the human corruption spawned by the struggle to survive. These people were just like Beth and I had been, growing more and more dependent on the UN for their daily survival. It was better than starving, I rationalized, but I knew from experience that doled out relief could come at a cost to the heart and soul. Who was ministering to all of these people in line? Who was telling them they still mattered? That all was not lost?

Farther on as we neared downtown Monrovia, traffic slowed to a crawl. Wary, vacant eyes stared into our car, especially at the curiosity of Bentley, a tall white man, riding next to me. One boy, who couldn't have been more than twelve or thirteen years old, stooped to peer into the back windows, a hand above his brow to shield his eyes from the sun's bright reflection on the glass. Rail-thin, he was dressed in dark sport shorts and a bright blue shirt, frayed sandals clinging to his mud-splattered feet. He carried a wooden tray piled high with small boxes of cereal, nuts, and other sundry items.

He was a street vendor.

We didn't stop, but I turned my head to look back at the boy. It was like seeing an image of me twenty-five years before, except I saw something else in this boy's narrow-eyed expression—a callousness and disregard for life, a numbness spawned by fear.

I also noticed a lethal-looking knife poking out from one of his pockets. This was apparently the new street reality here, the calculus of killing an equation solved only by the survivors. Goods were always for sale, but life itself was only worth so much.

CHAPTER THIRTY-THREE

The Place They Heard About

Wankollie woke us early the next morning, and a driver took us into Monrovia again. This morning, however, I had a particular destination in mind. At the ELWA junction, we turned west on the main road and headed into the neighborhood known as Congo Town.

Everywhere were more scenes of carnage. Burned-out cars and trucks. The shells of abandoned and bullet-riddled buildings interspersed with ramshackle newer structures. Laundry hung out on crumbling balconies and smashed-out window frames indicated people were still living in the skeletal remains of those shattered buildings.

I felt the same sense of despair in the air we'd witnessed the day before. You could see it in people's eyes as we passed, even in the way our driver gripped the steering wheel, not a casual way of controlling the vehicle, but a purposeful, wary holding on with a readiness to react to anything.

"These guys aren't exactly making it easy for people to move around," Bentley commented as we slowed for yet another UN checkpoint.

"I think that's the point," I said.

"At least they're not shooting at anybody—yet!" our driver muttered under his breath.

Who could blame the man for his cynicism? I thought back to when Doe was in charge. All his political machinations and whipsaw public proclamations, coupled with deep prejudices and hatred, had simply wrought tribal genocide and ruination. And his downfall had been followed by another dangerous leader in Charles Taylor. The evidence of their misrule was all around us.

As we waited in the line of vehicles, I pointed out to Bentley a large structure rising out of swampland. The Ministry of Defense building was an impressive monolithic edifice with elegant support columns comprised of curving concrete. While the project had never been completed, in my day it had been a structure in which Monrovians took great pride. The majestic facade was now pocked with bullet holes and blackened by the burning scars of war.

After making it through the checkpoint, our driver sped up as we entered Monrovia's Sinkor district.

"So where exactly are we going?" Bentley asked.

"There's a place I want to show you," I said. "We're almost there."

A minute later, the triangular roofline of St. Peter's Lutheran Church appeared ahead; I asked our driver to slow down and find a place to park.

"This is it?" Bentley asked. "The church?"

I nodded, hit with a sudden wave of memory and fear at

the sight of the building. No Liberian would ever forget what had happened here any more than Americans would forget the events of 9/11. It was the day that the perception of Liberia by foreign governments and most around the world had forever changed.

Our driver found a place to park. Climbing out of the vehicle, Bentley and I approached the church. This was a place I had passed hundreds of times while living in Monrovia without giving it a second thought. After becoming a Christian, I'd even attended a service or two here.

Now the structure looked in desperate need of renovation. All the glass in the windows had been shot out, and dark stains shadowed the exterior walls. Half a dozen UN vehicles were parked out front, and a number of officials were passing in and out of the entrance. A small crowd had gathered outside, including what looked to be a news crew, one with a camera taking photos while another appeared to be shooting a video. These people had all come here to see the building they'd heard or read so much about in the news, in much the same way Americans were drawn to visit Ground Zero in New York City, site of the Twin Towers before the 9/11 attacks.

CHAPTER THIRTY-FOUR

No Place to Hide

By July 30, 1990, Beth and I made it to the home of a pastor friend in Gaynah's Town, a small village some miles outside the city. At least for the time being, we were safe.

That had not been the case when stopped to rest at what we'd hoped would be the sanctuary of the University of Liberia's Fendell Campus two days earlier. It hadn't taken long to realize that the campus had morphed into a sort of death camp. Thousands of people were crammed onto the university grounds without running water, electricity, or any reliable source for food. The dead lay decomposing in the sun. A nearby creek had become filled with human waste. Rebels continued to roam at will among the refugees, hunting for anyone they felt might be even remotely affiliated with Doe's government or disloyal to Charles Taylor.

I knew Gaynah's Town well from working there as an evangelist before completing college. Pastor Dickson and his wife Ma Musu ministered at the local church. I was relieved to find them still alive and their small mud home still intact. They immediately took us in and gave us some food and fresh water.

That morning, however, I saw anxiety written all over the faces of those of us gathered around a radio to listen to the BBC daily news. Rumors were swirling through the town about a mass killing by government soldiers the night before. Could the rumors be true? What was happening to our once-proud little nation of Liberia?

Pastor Dickson waited until it was time for the BBC program before loading batteries into his transistor radio. With electricity to the area cut off and batteries hard to replace, everyone was carefully rationing their use. Once the BBC broadcaster came on the air, he confirmed our worst fears. A terrible massacre had taken place the night before at St. Peter's Lutheran Church in Monrovia.

The church was being used as an International Red Cross shelter for over two thousand refugees, including many Gio and Mano people, tribes targeted by President Doe and his soldiers for supporting the rebels. Despite the Red Cross flags flying all around the walled-in courtyard, soldiers from Doe's army had broken into the church, wielding machetes and firing machine guns. They singled out Gio and Mano men, women, and children.

"Bodies were everywhere," one witness had told news crews. "We were crawling over them. We were all just running and looking for some place to hide."

But there was nowhere left to hide. By the time all was said and done, the soldiers had massacred over six hundred Liberian civilians. The BBC announcer went on to talk about the international horror and outrage over the event. Most of us sat looking at one another in shock. Some averted their eyes and shook their heads, crying, especially those who feared they may have known some of the people in the church.

By now, we'd heard and seen enough atrocities being committed in this war, but to break into a church? To spill so much blood in a place consecrated to worship God? How could our fellow Liberians have done such a monstrous thing?

Beth and I were also angry. The BBC had reported the day before that the United States government had sent a shipload of US Marines to Monrovia and that the ship had arrived to help evacuate US Embassy personnel. We knew little about American foreign policy and nothing about the orders the Marines might have been given. All we knew was that as Liberians we'd been taught the basics of American history in school, which always included the idea that America was in some way our benefactor, our great Uncle Sam. How could US Marines have sat on their ship in the harbor just offshore while Doe's out-of-control Liberian Army committed such an atrocity?

Over the next few weeks, I joined Dickson in preaching the gospel and sharing God's love with suffering people hungry for hope as well as food. It wasn't easy to find a balance between dealing with the trauma of all the horrors going on around us while trying to reassure people that God was still in control. Every few days, Beth, Ma Musu, Dickson, and I would venture back onto the Fendell Campus, distributing food and other supplies while looking for any relatives or friends we might be able to help.

But food soon became scarce. None of us had much to eat, and Beth and I were both shedding pounds. I also started growing a long beard on the advice of a few rebel young men who, in a shock to all of us, had come to hear me preach. This was because clean-shaven adult men were suspected of being recruits for Doe's army; Taylor's rebels would often shoot such men on sight.

***

During the weeks we spent in Gaynah's Town with Pastor Dickson and Ma Musu, the fighting continued throughout Liberia. The rebels gained more and more territory in and around Monrovia. Then on September 10, we learned via the BBC that rebel soldiers had managed to trick President Samuel Doe into leaving the relative safety of his executive mansion for supposed peace talks. The soldiers were under the command of Prince Y. Johnson, leader of a splinter group called the INPFL that had broken away from Taylor's NPFL. After killing Doe's bodyguards, Johnson tortured and then executed the captured Liberian president. Johnson, savagely, even managed to video and broadcast the presidential "execution" for all the world to see.

The horrors continued.

With Doe's death, Liberia was thrust even deeper into chaos and civil war. The main rebel force under Charles Taylor moved to take over the country and consolidate their control. Some of the SIM missionaries who operated the ELWA radio station were forced by Taylor's rebels to get the facility back up and running, which Taylor was now using to broadcast his propaganda across the country.

Daniel, a close friend of ours, was one of the missionary engineers forced back to work. Because the rebels needed him, Daniel was given freedom to travel. Once he learned Beth and I were in Gaynah's Town, he came to see us.

I cried out in joy, happy to see him alive as he exited the ELWA van in which he'd pulled up outside Pastor Dickson's hut.

"Tony!" Daniel embraced me warmly. "I'm so glad you and your family are safe. How are Beth and the baby?"

"They are okay for now, thank God."

He went on to tell me how he'd been virtually kidnapped by Taylor and the rebels and taken back to ELWA to help get the station back on the air. Because they needed him healthy to support the broadcast facility, the rebels provided him with rice and some meat. He was currently staying in Kakata, a village about twenty miles away, traveling back and forth each day with a few other radio station personnel.

"What about the region upcountry?" I asked. "Has there been any word from the missionaries based near Balumah?"

"Balumah Belle? That's where you're from, isn't it? No, I'm sorry, Tony, we've heard no word at all from that area. But I'll ask around. Your family's Mandingo, right?"

"My mother is Mandingo, yes. My Belle father passed away a few years ago."

"I'll see what I can find out. But I'm sorry to say, if your mother's Mandingo ... well, you know what the rebels will do if they find her."

"Yes, I know."

"Monrovia is still very dangerous as well. The rebels protect us out at ELWA because they need us, but that doesn't mean they don't still come under attack. Some days, I'm not sure if I'm going to make it back to where I'm staying. At least things are safer in Kakata." Daniel left with an offer to provide transportation for Beth, Abigail, and me if we'd like to join him in Kakata.

The fighting continued all over Liberia as various rebel factions contended for territory. The ECOMOG (Economic Community of West African States Monitoring Group), a relatively small, multilateral peacekeeping army made up of forces from various West African nations, predominately Nigeria, had been sent in by the United Nations to help bring stability, but it had had little effect. Trucks full of young men with guns roared through Gaynah's Town at every hour. We could hear machine gun fire and explosions throughout the night.

For the baby's safety, Beth and I decided to take Daniel up on his offer. On September 21st, we packed up our few possessions and little Abigail, said goodbye to our dear friends, Pastor Dickson and his wife, and climbed into Daniel's van.

***

Kakata is a small city in the heart of Liberia's rubber-producing region not far from the massive Firestone rubber plantation. It is also home to the Booker Washington Institute, the country's first public agricultural and vocational college. By the time we arrived, Kakata had become an important regional headquarters for Charles Taylor's invading rebel fighters. For the time being, Daniel had found us a tiny one-bedroom apartment on the BWI campus. We were grateful, though still anxious about what might come next.

A close friend from Africa Bible College, whom we called Bongoma, was also living in Kakata at this time. He wasn't Liberian but from Ghana. Even with Doe gone, Charles Taylor was having trouble consolidating his power throughout the country. To complicate matters further, the ECOMOG peacekeeping force, ostensibly operating under the authority of the UN, had itself been drawn into the war. Charles Taylor and his rebel army had been fighting with the mostly Nigerian forces over control of certain territory and military assets. In consequence, Taylor had concluded that any non-Liberian Africans must be spies conspiring against him. If his rebels discovered that Bongoma was Ghanaian, he would be killed.

After praying and consulting with Daniel, Beth and I offered to hide Bongoma in our tiny apartment. This, of course, placed us at risk too if the rebels found out who he was.

"You don't have to do this, Tony," Bongoma told me. "You have a wife and a child."

"God will watch over us," I assured him. I believed my words, but even as I said them, fear stalked my heart, and I cried out silently in prayer for Jesus to give us all strength and protection.

For the next two months, Bongoma never left our apartment for fear of his life. He slept on our floor and shared whatever food we had to eat. We kept the shades drawn to keep him from being discovered. Meanwhile, just as in Gaynah's Town, conditions began to worsen. Food and water became even scarcer.

Then the local rebels, who were assigned to guard a large weapons depot, began evacuating their supplies. Rumors of an imminent attack began circulating throughout Kakata. Chaos and confusion were rampant as the local populace, including some of the remaining missionaries among whom we were living, began to flee.

What were Beth and I going to do? Abigail was eating a little better than she had in Gaynah's Town, but she was still weak and slept fitfully much of the time. Due to malnutrition,

Beth and I were continuing to lose strength as well; I could see the bones in Beth's wrist, and when I looked at my own limbs, I realized my arms and legs were atrophied shadows of what they'd been in my soccer playing days. We were often hungry, and sometimes the lack of food made it difficult to think clearly.

Some of Beth's extended family and others we knew and trusted had decided to travel to the city of Gbarnga, the capital of Bong County about seventy miles northeast of Monrovia. Gbarnga was the main headquarters for Charles Taylor's rebel army and less than a hundred miles from Yekepa, where I'd gone to college. It was also close to the border between Liberia and the Ivory Coast.

Beth and I were told we'd be welcome to travel with the group, but we worried about Bongoma. Could we simply pick up and go, leaving him behind? On the other hand, traveling with Bongoma might magnify the risk. What if bringing him meant we wouldn't be able to reach Gbarnga?

Holding hands, Beth and I prayed together. In the course of our prayers, I heard the Holy Spirit telling me that we must not leave Bongoma behind, but my faith wasn't strong enough. I needed reassurance, so I looked to Beth.

"Should we take Bongoma with us?" I asked. "What should we do?"

A power greater than her own seemed to fill my wife's countenance in that moment. Straightening her back, she looked at me directly. "Let's do it!"

As a pastor friend of mine often jokes, God's voice sounded very much like my wife's in that moment.

When the time came for us to leave and we were packing up the vehicles that had been arranged for the trip, Bongoma was with us. I made brief eye contact with a couple of the others who knew Bongoma's situation, fearing they might object. But God must have been working in their hearts as well because no one complained. In that moment, it didn't matter what tribe or country we were from. We were all refugees together.

***

Friends eventually found a house in Gbarnga where we could all stay. The house seemed like a palace compared to what we'd been used to, with four bedrooms, running water, and working toilets. It was also surrounded by fruit trees and a tall hedge that blocked out much of the outside world. Since Bong County was Charles Taylor's stronghold, we knew that we were living in the shadow of a warlord. But we also felt safer than we had in months.

Other refugees came and went, so we often had people sleeping in the other bedrooms, though sometimes we had the place to ourselves. Over the next few weeks, we stayed inside the property, except when I went out to look for food. We filled our time reading, playing games, and tending to Abigail, who'd begun to walk and was steadily progressing into toddlerhood. As new parents do, we worried over every little thing, especially how all the trauma and malnourishment might be hurting her development.

We were still hungry much of the time. I was also growing restless, feeling as though we were stuck in some temporary way station. In the middle of what would become known as the First Liberian Civil War, who could have imagined then how many years the power struggles, destruction, and killings would go on?

Each day, we put batteries into a table radio that came with the house to listen to the BBC news. Across Liberia, random pockets of fighting continued to rage, and resistance remained fierce as the Nigerian peacekeepers fought with Taylor's troops and other rebels to bring contested territory under ECOMOG control.

Being a pastor, I tried not to get too caught up in the politics of it all. I'd made that mistake years before while still a Muslim and in high school, getting drawn into the Marxist philosophies and politics of some of the professors and resistance leaders at the University of Liberia. Jesus had never tried to raise an army to attack Jerusalem or Rome. His concern was with people's hearts and with bearing witness to the truth of God's love and grace. That was what had changed in me when I accepted him into my life. Righting social wrongs through social change was a desirable and sometimes noble thing, but only Jesus had the power to permanently change people's hearts. Only Jesus had the power to drive out fear.

Even in my growing restlessness, I took time to read and study the Bible. More and more, I felt God's Spirit telling me that perhaps the time had come for Beth, Abigail, and me to leave Liberia. My ministry to Muslims through ELWA was over. ELWA's evangelistic programming had ceased to be broadcast into West Africa, and outside of the skeletal crew keeping broadcasts going on behalf of the rebels, the entire ELWA campus had been severely damaged or destroyed. The hospital and the school were no more, and the foreign missionaries had all been evacuated. With communication virtually at a standstill, no one knew what had become of the rest of the scattered Liberian ELWA personnel.

I wish I could say my trust in God remained strong in the

face of such adversity, but the truth is that my faith wavered at times, and I even began to have doubts about God's purpose for my life. I was careful not to share too many of these thoughts with Beth or others. We'd seen so much senseless killing, seen so much horror and destruction. We were just trying to survive day by day. I still believed in God, but I kept asking myself how a loving creator could allow such things to happen to my family and my country? How could God allow such insanity and evil to flourish and men seemingly turned into animals?

Looking back, I allowed other seeds of bitterness to erode my faith as well. As the BBC informed us, America and Americans were caught up in the tension and drama of the First Gulf War against Iraq with over thirty-five coalition nations taking part in Operation Desert Storm to expel Saddam Hussein's Iraqi troops from their occupation of Kuwait. The fighting and suffering in tiny Liberia was little more than a provincial asterisk to such global power struggles. There were no live CNN broadcasts from the front lines documenting the horrors and atrocities committed by Charles Taylor's teenage rebel army and so many others here. Even when reports did make the international news, the world seemed to be turning a blind eye to our suffering. For those of us on the ground in Liberia, however, there was no way to escape the starvation and peril.

***

As Christmas 1990 approached, hunger continued to be a problem in Gbarnga, and people had little to give. Among the few remaining missionaries, we were hoping for at least some semblance of a Christmas celebration. Our hopes were dashed a week before Christmas, however, when we heard the unmistakable approaching roar of Nigerian Air Force Russian-designed jet bombers. Seconds later, they swooped over our house and the treetops of Gbarnga like a high-speed avalanche of thunder.

Stepping outside, I caught a glimpse of three sleek shapes passing like shadows overhead through the bright sky. They dropped no bombs that first day, but we could hear sporadic gunfire aimed at the jets coming from across the city. Everyone seemed to understand what the flyover portended. It was as if the pilots had broadcast a warning: *We're coming. Best you leave now!*

And come they did. Where were we to go?

The next morning, the planes returned, and this time they were loaded with bombs. Explosions rocked the small city. Smoke rose all around our temporary house, and the building felt like it was about to be knocked off its foundation.

I can't remember how many attack runs the bombers made, but it seemed to last forever. The attackers targeted Taylor's command post and barracks as well as the city marketplace. Hundreds died, including many civilians. When it was finally over, Beth and I stood holding on to one another in the kitchen, cradling Abigail in our arms as she wailed in terror.

"We have to get out of here," I said. "We need to get to the Ivory Coast."

Once again, we packed up our meager belongings, and I went to secure exit papers for us. Bongoma had already left the city a few days before. He'd approached us a couple of weeks earlier to tell us he no longer wished to endanger us. He'd decided to cross the border into the Ivory Coast alone, hoping to escape that way back to his home country of Ghana. Through Beth's extended family, we'd helped him obtain exit papers we hoped might give him safe passage. We didn't know if he'd been able to safely navigate the ninety-mile journey to the border, but when the bombs began to fly, I was wishing we'd gone with him.

***

Still, instead of leaving right away, doubts clouded my mind, and I hesitated. Yes, we were in Gbarnga, Bong County, still keeping our heads down because this area was the head-quarters for Charles Taylor. Yes, Taylor's forces were under attack, but I changed my mind about going to Ivory Coast. I had a different idea about where we should go because, in spite of the way Mama had treated Beth and me, I still worried about her.

"I want to go back to Balumah," I told Beth. "We need to check on Mama."

"Balumah?" Beth said. "Are you crazy? Do you have any idea how dangerous that will be for all of us?"

"The road forks just north of here to take us back in the direction. It may take a week or so to get there, but I feel like we need to go."

"You always underestimate things. It may take weeks to get there with all of the fighting, if we even can. And what are you planning to do once you get there?"

"I don't know. I just want to find out if they're all right."

"Why must you know this, Tony? Your family has rejected you. Your mother has rejected me. You've done your best to reach out to them. There is nothing more you can do for your mother or your family now."

"I still want to go," I insisted.

"You don't even know if your family is there anymore," Beth pointed out. "And if we could make it to the village, the rebels there would probably kill you or capture you and force you into the fighting."

On and on we argued well into the night. I said some things I regret, and I'm sure Beth did as well. In the end, however, my beautiful wife wasn't budging.

"If you go to Balumah," she said finally, "Abigail and I can't go with you. We'll try to get out to Ivory Coast on our own."

"You *what*? What are you saying?"

"You have to choose between us and your family, Tony. We are your family now. It's as simple as that."

I don't know if I've ever felt angrier than I did at that moment. I sat in stony silence for what must have been only a couple of minutes, but seemed like hours. What more could I say? Why did I feel so drawn to reconnect with Mama and my family despite all that had happened and the danger involved?

I realized it was because of something unique to Jesus I'd never found in Islam: a relationship. I didn't follow Jesus in the same way I used to follow Muhammad as a Muslim. Unlike Islam and Judaism and every other world religion, the power of the gospel of Jesus Christ didn't stem from the traditions and teachings of religion, even the religion we call Christianity. There were no traditions of Jesus for me to follow or five pillars of Christianity.

Instead, through God's grace, I'd been granted salvation through the power of his Son and the Holy Spirit. This relationship was what the concept of the Trinity was all about. I had a personal relationship with Jesus, and the power in following Jesus stemmed from being in relationship with his supernatural Spirit that still lives and breathes and speaks and moves in the lives of millions of believers every day.

The fact that Mama and the rest of my family had rejected Jesus and rejected me had no impact on my continued desire for relationship with them. Through my faith in Jesus, I still had a deep love for my mother no matter how she might have treated my wife or me. Our different faiths aside, nothing would ever change the fact that God had given me an earthly mother, father, and family and that God's desire was for our relationship to be healed.

But God was also reminding me he'd given to me a wise and godly wife and at times a vital counselor. He had blessed our relationship. God himself had given in Scripture the instruction for man to leave his father and mother to be joined to his wife (Genesis 2:24; Ephesians 5:31). That meant I was to choose my wife over my family.

"Are you okay, Tony?" Beth must have thought I'd gone into some sort of a trance.

"I'm all right. Just thinking and praying."

"What are you going to do?"

"I'm not going to leave you and Abigail alone. I know that much," I said. "All right. We'll go to Ivory Coast."

CHAPTER THIRTY-FIVE

We Are Finished

On my third day back in Liberia, I arose before Bentley woke up and went out on my own. I was beginning to feel a bit more comfortable despite the devastation, and since things had seemed relatively safe so far, I decided to venture on foot toward the suburbs.

I was walking near Duport Road when someone recognized me.

"Tony Weedor?"

"Yes?"

"Do you remember me?"

I looked the man over. He was a heavyset fellow with a kindly smile that was missing some teeth. "I'm sorry. I don't remember you, my friend."

"That's okay, it's been a long time. The last time I saw you was in Bomi during the first war. I heard you preach. Someone told us you tried to get to Gbarnga. We all thought you were dead."

"So I've been told."

"Where are you living now?

"America. Colorado."

"Really? Colorado. I've heard they have snow there."

"Yes. It gets very cold."

He laughed. "I'd like to see that sometime. Hey—do you have any American cash on you? Do you think you could help me out?"

"Sorry, my friend, I don't have any money." I turned out my empty pockets to show him.

The man looked disappointed, but his smile didn't waver. He stared at me as though I were some alien being and not the same man he'd heard preaching. I felt out of place.

I passed another man on my walk that I vaguely remembered. He stared at me in awkward silence then reached out tentatively to shake my hand as though making sure I was whom he thought I was. Maybe for both men it was as if a lost piece of their past had somehow been brought back to life, and my unlikely return meant their own lost loved ones might one day do the same.

My sister Victoria arrived later that morning. I recognized her immediately as she stepped down from one of the few public buses still operating in Monrovia.

"Tony?"

"Vickie! You made it." I broke into a grin.

"It's really you." She burst into sobs.

I reached out to embrace her, and for a long moment she hung on to me as though she might take some tangible solace from my physical presence. I felt the pain of our shared history buried beneath years of anger and estrangement, morphed by terror, war, and horrors the likes of which neither of us could have ever imagined.

"Are you real?" She put a hand on my cheek.

I nodded.

"I can hardly believe you're here."

I was shocked at how much she'd changed. We were about the same age—mid-forties—but though her features were still attractive, they were severely lined, and her body had clearly suffered the effects of malnutrition.

"Are you okay?" I asked.

"Not really," she said. She rubbed one arm as if she were in pain or nervous in my presence. "It's just … well, it's pretty overwhelming to see you again after all of this time."

"Thank you so much for coming."

"When I heard you'd be here and wanted to try to reunite with Mama, I had to come."

"Will Mama meet with me?"

"Maybe. I hope so." She gave a little shrug. "We'll have to see."

The war seemed to have taken a toll on her spirit as well. Post traumatic stress disorder was too genteel a label to describe what I saw in her eyes. They bore a haunting reflection of horrors remembered. Anger and fear seemed to have melted in her into the beaten down resignation of one for whom physical and emotional peril had become a constant reality.

Victoria walked with me back to the ELWA guesthouse where Wankollie had brought food and water for us and laid it out on a table. I introduced her to Bentley. Then we sat outside on stools, looking out at the ocean, eating, and talking for a couple of hours. I asked her about a number of our friends and acquaintances, many of whom she told me were either dead or gone. I asked her about Mama.

"Mama is very depressed," she said. "She's been under so much strain, I don't know how she survives. We are finished."

"What do you mean?" I asked.

"We are finished as a nation, Tony. Everything is destroyed. Even the ELWA hospital here is in ruins. This is not the Liberia you once knew, as you've probably seen. So many thousands of us have died. Many others fled like you. The UN soldiers are here, and that is good, but that hasn't completely stopped the killing or the danger. Everyone here is basically out for him or herself."

There was so much I wanted to tell Victoria about Jesus, and about God's love and grace, but now was not the time. She needed a sympathetic listening ear, not a sermon.

"Do you have any news about our village?" I asked. "What's been happening in Balumah?"

"The rebels drove Doe's forces out of that area quite some time ago. Mama and the family are gone, scattered, most of them now here like the rest of the refugees. We've heard things have been very bad in Balumah since Taylor's rebels took over. Almost everyone else we used to know is gone. Terrible things have happened there—even back before you escaped from Liberia. You heard about what happened to our cousin, Emanuel Kollie, didn't you?"

"No, I haven't heard. Please, tell me." All I remembered of my cousin was a bright young man who'd gone off to Monrovia and taken a job working for the government.

"He left Monrovia to come back to Balumah because he wanted to get away from the fighting. He thought it would be safe for him there, but he was wrong. He walked right into an ambush. The rebels murdered him."

Her words brought to mind the argument I'd gotten into

with Beth years before and how badly I'd wanted to go back to Balumah even in the middle of the war. Beth had given me an ultimatum and finally convinced me not to go. It turned out she'd been right. Through Beth's resolve, God may have saved all of our lives that day.

Later, after we were all talked out, I walked Victoria back up to the main road to catch the bus. The air was thick with humidity, insects buzzed like flying bullets, and the afternoon sun had just begun to sink behind a line of trees. Soon I saw the bus approaching. I turned to my sister. "I really appreciate you coming out here today to catch me up on things, Vickie."

"I'm glad I did. With so much that has happened, I think maybe it's finally time. Mama has had to struggle to stay alive, just like the rest of us. But she isn't young anymore. I'm really hoping she will be willing to see you."

"Me, too."

"She said if I saw you to make sure I touched you. I think she wonders if you might actually be some kind of a spirit."

"Well, now you can tell her not to worry. I'm still flesh and bones."

"I will."

"How about if I try to come see Mama the day after tomorrow?"

"I'll ask. You know Mama though."

Yes, I knew Mama all right. But how well can you really know someone you haven't seen for so long?

The bus stopped in front of us and the door opened. Moving toward it, Victoria's face went blank as if she were steeling her will for reentry into a world of fear and uncertainty. Turning back to look at me, she waved and gave me a small smile before climbing aboard for her ride home.

CHAPTER THIRTY-SIX

You Are Dead

By early 1991, we were standing on the banks of the Cavalla River just across the water from Ivory Coast. We were ready to cross the border, and by then I'd come to the realization it was my fear of separation and anger at Mama and the rest of my family that had caused me to be so angry with Beth back in Gbarnga. It felt strange to be leaving our homeland and families behind, but my anger had also evolved into a bitterness toward Liberia, toward the murder, hatred, and insanity, and toward the warlords and their ignorant boy soldiers who had taken so much from us and our fellow countrymen.

We were treated kindly at the border crossing by the Ivory Coast soldiers. Walking out of the Ivorian immigration office, I turned to take one last look across the river at Liberia, then proclaimed to my wife and another missionary who was traveling with us, "I will never set foot back onto that land again." They laughed, thinking I was making a joke, but at that time I meant every word.

We soon came to realize, however, that crossing a border into another country didn't mean we'd escaped our situation as refugees. None of us spoke French, the predominant language in Ivory Coast. Everything seemed different, and though we'd managed to hide some money in our clothing to keep the Liberian rebels guarding the border from seizing it, we had very few resources and no way of supporting ourselves.

We'd been directed to go to a large UN refugee camp outside Abidjan, where we were told we'd find shelter and adequate food. I soon learned Beth, Abigail, and I were only one tiny family in a sea of humanity, a massive West African diaspora made up of more than three hundred thousand people, mostly Liberians fleeing the fighting, destruction, and starvation surrounding the civil war.

With other refugees, we rode on a bus for what seemed like hours. By the time we arrived outside Abidjan, we were exhausted and hungry. The Liberian rebel soldiers at the border had confiscated most of our belongings, so we had few possessions to our name. We thought about going directly to the UN camp, but we'd also heard about an old friend of mine from ELWA mission, Bruce Penkie, who'd escaped to the Ivory Coast early in the fighting and was living somewhere nearby. After several inquiries and false starts, we finally found Bruce's house.

"Tony and Beth Weedor? I can't believe my eyes!" Our old friend ran out to greet us and embrace us when we appeared on his front porch.

"Hello, Bruce," I said. "You don't know how good it feels to see you."

"I'm just glad it really is you. I barely recognized you with the beard, plus you've lost so much weight. But more than that, I received a newsletter only two days ago from SIM in Liberia with news about many of the ELWA missionaries. The letter said you and your family are dead." Bruce showed me the piece of paper.

I smiled widely. "Well, I don't know where they're getting their information these days, but as you can see, it's incorrect."

"I know, I know, it's just such good news I can still hardly believe it! Come in! Come in! Let me see if we can get you all something to eat."

***

We soon found a temporary place to stay with another missionary friend. Some time later, I ran into Bruce again on my way to search for supplies. This time, Bruce and I sat on a bench beneath a tree and talked more about what was happening in Liberia. Despite international efforts by the UN and others, the fighting and killing had continued.

"I'm so thankful you and Beth and the baby got out, Tony. It's a miracle, really. I hear from those few remaining at the mission that things are growing worse all the time. No food and no electricity. No clean water. Turns out, Taylor's rebels are as bad as Doe's army when it comes to butchering people. Maybe worse."

"I'm still worried about my family in Balumah," I said. "My mother and my brothers and one of my sisters are still there. My uncle Sekou is the local imam."

"Balumah? Sekou?" Bruce's expression darkened.

"What's wrong?" I asked.

"I passed through there last year and spoke with some of the people. The rebels were in control. It was very bad."

"What do you mean?"

He took a deep breath. "I hate to have to be the one to tell you this, my friend. I don't know anything about your mother, but I heard from more than one person about the local Muslim imam, a man named Sekou.

"Yes. That's my uncle. Please go on."

"Well, I was told by many that the rebels tied your uncle together with all of his wives, marched them into a field at gunpoint, and made them lie down next to one another. Then the rebels poured gasoline all over them and burned them alive."

It took a moment for Bruce's words to sink in.

"I'm so sorry, Tony."

All I could think of was walking with Uncle Sekou through the fields as a teenager while he taught me verses from the Quran. I'd so looked up to him then, and though he'd long since rejected me for becoming a Christian and rebuffed my efforts to communicate with him about Jesus, I still loved my uncle. I'd even dreamed that one day I'd be able to reach him with the gospel, and that he would come to know the love of Jesus as I had.

I choked back tears.

"Are you all right?" Bruce asked.

"Yes," I said, although I really wasn't.

"Again, I'm so sorry."

Later that night, something came over me I'd never experienced before. The world seemed to grow completely dark. I can only describe it as a deep depression. Maybe I was suffering from malnutrition or it was a delayed reaction to the trauma we'd suffered, coupled with the sudden realization we didn't have to be in constant fear for our lives anymore.

Beth felt it, too. I remember hearing gunfire on one of our first nights in the Ivory Coast, huddling with Beth and Abigail in the corner of our bedroom all night long, being afraid to move, and wondering what was going on. The next day, we found out the shooting was just part of a routine Ivorian army training.

***

Within a few days, we moved into the UN refugee camp. I felt deeply depressed; I wasn't even sure I ever wanted to preach again. In contrast, Beth's mood seemed to improve. She tried to encourage me, but I was having none of it, so my wise wife came up with an idea.

"We need to start a Bible study," she told me.

"Where?"

"Here in the camp."

"What?" I looked around at the squalor of the sea of tents. "Have you lost your mind?"

You can still find pictures on the internet of the camp for Liberian refugees in Ivory Coast where Beth, Abigail, and I spent much of the next two years. Row upon row of curved wooden frames, on the tops of which are lashed thick, tan colored tarps bearing the sky blue logo of the UN's international refugee program. Packed brown earth without a blade of green. Sometimes earnest, sometimes empty black faces with sad, staring eyes.

But a snapshot in time only encapsulates a miniscule fraction of our experiences. The raw smells of human waste, cooking fires, and animal excrement are lost to the camera. So is the punishing heat of the tropical African sun. The drenching monsoon rains setting tents afloat and turning the ground to muddy rivers. The constant swarms of fruit flies.

Not to mention the anxiety and gnawing uncertainties of barely adequate food supplies and health care. The corruption and stealing of food by officials and others. The bartering of human flesh in a thriving sex trade.

These are the realities the self-congratulatory photos on UN websites too often fail to portray. These are the realities with which we, the inhabitants of such camps, had to contend each and every day.

"I'm not organizing or speaking to any Bible study here," I told Beth.

"Oh, yes you are. You have to. You need a purpose. Let's start right away."

I needed to find a way to get my wife to stop bothering me so I could wallow some more in my depression. I thought of a way.

"I won't talk to anyone unless there are more than twenty-five people," I said, feeling smug.

I knew this was next to impossible. We'd only just moved into the camp and knew no one. But I was underestimating God and my wife.

Two nights later, nearly thirty people crowded in and around our tent to hear me, former Muslim now Pastor Tony Weedor from Balumah, talk about the Bible, faith, and all that we'd been through in Liberia. I guess we were all like desperate shipwrecked sailors lost on some strange island far from our homes.

Soon my depression began to lift. Our Bible study was growing. I wish I could take credit for some of this, but it was Beth who spread the message through word of mouth, speaking herself and organizing all of the women to reach out to more and more people. Within a few months after moving into the camp, those first seeds planted by Beth under the influence of the Holy Spirit had grown to a number of Bible studies spread throughout the sprawling refugee camp. Beth and I spoke to all of these "fellowships" as we'd started to call these Christian gatherings, rotating among them on a regular basis.

One day, I was standing by the door of a UN tent, waiting to be introduced by the occupant of the temporary dwelling to a group of forty or so young adults who'd gathered to hear me speak. My host finished his introduction, then invited me to move before the group to speak. I took a few steps out from the side of the tent to stand behind a makeshift lectern someone had erected out of crates.

"Ya, hello-o." I greeted everyone.

"Hello-o, Pastor," came the response.

Looking around the group, I recognized most if not all of the believers seated on tarps spread on the ground. But as I began speaking, I noticed a group of five late arrivals joining the crowd in back. The newcomers were all teenagers, a couple of whom wore gold chains and red bandanas; I instantly realized that these were young fighters who had been part of Charles Taylor's rebel army—the same type of rebels who had murdered my uncle.

A pit of fear welled up in my stomach. In my anxiety, I even imagined a couple of the young men even looked familiar. I couldn't be sure, but they may well have been among the so-called soldiers who'd terrorized our group and murdered so many when we were driven out of the ELWA campus. How was I to preach to such as these when they continued to spark such trauma in me? What could I possibly say?

I decided then and there to turn everything over to the Holy Spirit. I can't even remember what I said that day to the gathered group. I hope it was helpful. I only know that it was not I but God who spoke through me to the brokenness and sin and evil that had brought so much pain and suffering upon us all. Toward the end, I remember looking at the young soldiers and seeing them not as monsters, but as searching souls just like me, confused and hungry for the truth.

***

Early one morning, Beth and I were preparing a meal of rice and vegetables in our tent when Dr. Larry Tiedje appeared in our doorway.

"You're back!" I exclaimed.

"Good morning, Beth and Tony! So good to see you!"

Larry was a practicing dentist from the United States whom we'd known in Liberia. We hadn't known him well back in Liberia, but had come to know him very well here in the camp. Larry and his wife Linda were long-time SIM missionaries to Liberia who had been evacuated by the mission to Ivory Coast where they continued to serve the growing Liberian refugee population.

By this time, we'd been in the refugee camp for more than two years ourselves. (We'd celebrated our daughter Abigail's fourth birthday in our UN-issued tent.) Larry had been very supportive of my preaching and our church planting ministry of growing fellowships within the camp. He'd just returned from the US, where he'd been on furlough.

We embraced and shook hands. Then Larry asked how we'd

been getting along. We told him how we were okay healthwise; Abigail was getting bigger every day; and God was continuing to bless our tent fellowship ministry. "Tell me," he asked, "how has the food distribution been going?"

While still in the Ivory Coast, Larry had coordinated a large distribution of food that went beyond what was provided by the UN, all donated through his church and other Christian organizations for the refugees in the camps. When he'd left to go on furlough, he'd put Beth and me in charge of this food allotment and distribution, a big responsibility we'd felt humbled to take on.

"Everything seems to be going well," I told him. "A few problems, but we've been able to work things out."

"So I hear. And I know how much work it is. I'm so appreciative of you and Beth." Larry put his hand on my shoulder. "Tony, Beth, I have something important to talk with you about … What if I were to tell you I might have found a way out for you?"

"A way out?"

"A way out of the camp. A way to further develop your preaching and your ministry."

"Where would we go?"

"To America."

"America!" I didn't want to let myself believe it might be true. Like many other Liberians, Beth and I had long dreamed of traveling to or even moving to America. Despite our frustrations over the failure of the United States to intervene at critical times during the civil war, that dream was still alive and well. "That would be amazing, but what exactly are you speaking of?"

"Seminary. I have some friends from a church in Colorado

who said they might be willing to sponsor you to attend a wonderful school there—Denver Theological Seminary."

"What about Beth and Abigail? I can't go without them. Will they be able to go to America?"

"Why not?" he said. "But you'll have to be accepted to the seminary. I can get you an application and you may need to study to pass the entrance exam."

"Of course. I can hardly believe the words you are saying."

"I'll stop by again in the next few days with some more information and ask them to send me an application."

"Thank you, Larry. Thank you so much."

"Thank the Lord, not me. It looks like He may be making a way."

"This is so exciting!" Beth said. "I can hardly believe it either."

Beth and I and little Abigail held hands and danced around our tent in joy.

CHAPTER THIRTY-SEVEN

Into the Sun

The following afternoon, Bentley and I were driven around Monrovia, visiting many of the places where I'd once gone to school and worked. Monrovia Central High, now deserted, was a shell of its former self, covered in graffiti and bullet holes, its courtyard littered by chunks of broken concrete and shards of desks and chairs. The soccer goals were long gone, and huge puddles of water and mud covered the fields where I'd once played.

A few blocks away, Kumar's house was still standing, but it now belonged to someone else. His business and movie theater no longer existed; he'd sold them when he was forced to flee the country, and the building had been converted to some other purpose.

"What are you thinking?" Bentley asked as we surveyed the damage at a familiar intersection, once a thriving corner where I'd peddled my wares as a teen vender.

"It's all so sad. Like Victoria said, there's nothing left."

He nodded. "Makes me think of the destruction of Jerusalem from the Old Testament, a once great city brought to ruin."

"Yes, but what about all these people? The young men we see walking the streets—they are still like overgrown children. Where are the schools? Where is their education? They may know how to shoot a gun or swing a machete, how to fight and how to steal, but where does that leave them? Where are all of the businesses and companies that once invested here?"

"Moved to safer countries, I guess."

"How will all these people be fed then? Where are the jobs?"

Bentley raised an eyebrow. "The UN, I suppose."

"Yes. I suppose."

"Building peace, redevelopment—these all take time."

"Christ is what's really needed here," I said. "The work of the Holy Spirit in people's hearts."

On Broad Street, we were stopped in traffic for a moment in front of the burnt out remains of the four-story Ecobank. I could remember when this building housed a thriving enterprise where people from all over the world who lived in Monrovia kept and moved their money. Now people lived as squatters in the midst of the open steel girders that once formed the frame of the building. Laundry, stained sheets and towels, and even someone's collection of men's belts flapped in the breeze while vegetation sprouted from inside the structure with vines intertwining the support beams and bushes protruding from its sides.

The windowless monolith looked like some kind of grotesque, high-rise jail from an apocalyptic movie where people fought over the scraps of a civilization. Which I suppose in some ways it was. A hate-fueled warlord's jail. A drugged-out boy soldier's jail. A starving widow's jail. A corrupt official's jail. All in a nation—my nation—that had become a jail of its own making.

On Capitol Hill near the campus of the University of Liberia, we passed another badly damaged city building. But this structure was different than the others. As if mocking the reality of what had happened to Liberia, the words and inscriptions on the side of the building were still clearly visible.

TEMPLE OF JUSTICE
LET JUSTICE BE DONE TO ALL MEN

Carved into the stone above these words stood a large bas-relief image of the Liberian coat of arms. In between the two lines rested another bas-relief of the scales of justice. This was the home of Liberia's Supreme Court, although I doubted there'd been much activity here of late. The concrete was dirty and pockmarked with damage from the war, but the walls were still fairly intact, and someone had boarded up the large openings once filled by plate glass windows.

We kept going. Outside the US Embassy in the Mamba Point neighborhood, a dirty white concrete stairwell with a black wrought iron railing led up a steep bank to a soot-stained wall and the embassy itself, a recessed structure protected by an outer shell of concrete columns and lattice-like cross beams. US Marines armed with M-4s and wearing green fatigues, camouflage helmets, and dark glasses stood guard on the stairwell and perimeter, staring down at the traffic on United Nations Drive.

Looking through the fence at the embassy compound as we passed by, I was reminded once again of the stark contrast between our home in Colorado and this distant American outpost, this fortified pinpoint of sanity in a darkened city. On the roof of one of the embassy buildings, I spotted more soldiers manning a guard post piled high with sandbags. I'd been told the Marines deployed here called it Mamba Station, a play on the deadly nature of the mamba snake so common in Liberia. Their mission was simply to secure the embassy and embassy personnel, and they were under orders not to intervene in any simmering internal disputes between formerly warring Liberian factions. That was the job of the UN peacekeeping force.

Living in America for as long as I had, I recognized that the time for Africans to look to America or other Western powers to solve their problems was gone. Liberians would have to learn new and better ways to govern themselves without killing one another in the process. It wouldn't be easy.

One of the soldiers looking over the top of the sandbags made eye contact with me through our car window, no doubt to make sure I wasn't a threat. I suddenly felt sorry for these Marines on their rooftop; they were a long way from home.

Soon thereafter, Bentley and I got out of the car to walk around. Everywhere we went, people would look at us and point, especially at Bentley, wondering what this tall, white American was doing here. When word somehow began to spread that Bentley was a doctor, a small crowd of people looking for medical attention surrounded us. Bentley did his best to attend to a few needs, but since we hadn't come here on a medical mission, we had no supplies or equipment.

At the end of Broad Street, we wound uphill on the access road to the Ducor Palace Hotel. Perched on a beautiful promontory overlooking the city, the eight-story Ducor was once the epitome of African international class hotels. Built in the early 1960s, it boasted 106 luxury rooms, a beautiful outdoor swimming pool overlooking the Atlantic Ocean, and an elegant central lobby with a floating staircase. Unfortunately, all that remained now was the skeleton of the building shadowed by mold. Garbage and human waste littered the grounds and filled the swimming pool. Its destroyed glory seemed to symbolize all that'd been lost in Liberia and all that might have been.

As we left the hotel parking lot, an elderly couple approached us leading by the hand a man who looked to be in his late twenties or early thirties.

"Can you help us?" the old man asked. "We're looking for help for our son."

Bentley stopped to address them. "This is your son?"

"Yes. He used to be young and strong, but now he can no longer see."

"When did he lose his vision?"

"During the war."

Bentley turned to the son. "How did you become blind?"

In a halting voice, the younger man told us his story. When still a young teen toward the end of Doe's reign, he had been suspected by Doe's troops of being a rebel recruit. He'd been beaten and tortured for hours, but had refused to give the soldiers the names of any of his friends. So the soldiers had tied him to the ground on his back with his eyes propped open to stare into the sun. He'd been left like that for hours, permanently damaging his retinas.

With an earnest face, the man's elderly father looked to Bentley. "Please tell us, doctor. Can anything be done to help our son see? It's like he has lost his eyes to the sun. "

Bentley and I shared a glance. The look of sadness on Bentley's face said it all, and he took his time in answering. "I am very sorry, sir, for what happened to your son. Medically, the answer to your question is no. With so much damage to his eyes, I'm afraid there is nothing that can be done to restore his vision."

The father nodded, almost as if he'd been expecting such an answer, but had to ask it anyway.

"But we believe in a God of miracles, and we can pray," Bentley said. "Our God in Jesus Christ can do all sorts of miracles. Sometimes, they may include physical healing, sometimes not."

Mother and father and son all seemed to understand and nodded their heads in unison.

So pray we did, the five of us linking hands and bowing our heads on a hillside, looking out at a shattered city framed by a beautiful sea on a day when the blazing West African sun, once used by evil men to rob this family's son of his eyesight, floated high in a sky free of clouds.

CHAPTER THIRTY-EIGHT

Not Without Them

Inside our UN tent shelter, Dr. Larry Tiedje explained in more depth the opportunity that might take Beth, Abigail, and me out of that refugee camp as well as further my education. It involved applying to Denver Theological Seminary's (DTS) Master of Divinity (MDiv) program in Denver, CO. Assuming I was accepted, Larry explained that he had several contacts with a congregation there who might be able to help us with expenses, living arrangements, and other issues.

I'd always been a good student and had continued to diligently study the Bible after my graduation from African Bible College. Still, acceptance to DTS's prestigious and rigorous program seemed a big stretch for a Liberian "country people" like me. I had two big things on my side. I spoke English, and I believed with all my heart that God was for me. If God wanted me to serve him by continuing my education through this program, he would watch over and strengthen me.

Invigorated by the possibility of going to school in America, I went to work. After much correspondence back and forth, I managed to pull together my college transcripts and letters of recommendation. I wrote out my testimony and the required essays and put in my application. I will never forget the moment we received my acceptance letter from the seminary. Jumping for joy like children, Beth and I held hands with little Abigail and did a dance. Within just a few weeks, God seemed to be opening every door for us to go to America.

That is, until we arrived for our visa interview at the American embassy in Abidjan. This was an imposing rectangular building that stood well back of a fortified iron fence guarded by armed security forces as well as US Marines. Seated across a desk from me, the State Department officer in charge of approving visas for Liberian refugees appeared skeptical of my motives.

"So you're planning to go to seminary in Denver?" The woman's blonde hair was pulled back in a bun, and behind dark framed eyeglasses her eyes seemed filled with fatigue, wariness, and a knowing worldliness. Her question sounded more like a challenge than a request for information.

"Yes, ma'am," I told her.

"Can you prove you've been accepted to an accredited school?"

I produced a copy of my diploma from African Bible College along with letters of recommendation from my professors and my acceptance letter from DTS.

The immigration officer didn't seem all that impressed. No doubt she'd come across her share of falsified documents and refugees attempting all sorts of chicanery in order to obtain visas to travel to America. She reached into her bottom desk drawer. I was surprised to see her pull out a King James Bible and open it.

"Recite for me, please, the first five books of the Old Testament," she said.

What was this, an exam? But I did as the officer asked and began naming the books—Genesis, Exodus, Leviticus, Numbers, and Deuteronomy—even throwing in the next two books—Joshua and Judges—for good measure.

She stuck out her chin and nodded. "Impressive. Okay, when do you plan to begin your studies, and how are you planning to pay for your education?"

"I'm planning to begin my studies this fall. I'll be on scholarship and also doing work for the school to help pay my tuition."

"All right. Sounds like you have a good plan. But what about your wife and your young daughter left back here in Ivory Coast?"

"What?"

"The student visa only applies to you. What's going to happen to them back here while you're working toward your advanced degree in America?"

Perhaps it was my naiveté, but I'd never even considered the possibility that Beth and Abigail wouldn't be going with me. Up until then, I'd been breezing through the interview, but now I didn't know what to say. I felt disoriented with all of my dreams of going to study in America about to be dashed.

"Oh," I finally managed to splutter. "I assumed they'd be coming with me."

"Well, you assumed wrong."

I glanced through the open door of her office down the corridor where Beth had scooped up Abigail and was holding her in her lap. Our four-year-old daughter was staring intently into a picture book her mother held open, reflexively kicking one leg, as Beth patiently turned the pages.

"Not without them," I said to the consulate official.

She raised an eyebrow. "What do you mean?"

"I'm not going then. I'm not going to America to study unless my family can go too."

She stared at me for a long moment, almost as if she was trying to read my heart—which I suppose in retrospect maybe she was. "You're serious, aren't you?"

"Yes, ma'am."

She'd been leaning forward with her arms crossed on the desk, but now she leaned back in her chair, removed her eyeglasses, and rubbed at the corner of one eye before putting the glasses back on. "You know, you're the first Liberian man I've ever had come through here seeking a visa who wouldn't just take a visa for themselves alone."

I shrugged. "I can't speak for other men."

She let out a long breath and said nothing. I sat looking at her across the desk.

"All right, Pastor," she said finally. "I believe you. I'll grant you and your wife and daughter visas. Just don't make me regret it."

***

Our dream of coming to America finally came true on August 5, 1993, when we boarded an airliner in Abidjan bound for New York.

I wish I had space in this volume to tell you all about our first impressions of America, about arriving in New York City, and about enrolling in seminary in Colorado. I wish I could tell you about all of the wonderful church families and friends in Denver who "adopted" our family and helped us in so many ways to become acclimated to American culture. I wish I could tell you about our experiences after completing my seminary training of teaching and serving as missionaries in Ethiopia and the story of my long journey to become an American citizen.

But I'm afraid all those stories will have to wait for another book because the story of how my life changed coming back to Liberia to see Mama will more than fill the remainder of these pages.

CHAPTER THIRTY-NINE

Matavi

By 2004, like so many other Liberians forced into similar conditions, Mama had been reduced to living in a shantytown outside Monrovia called Matavi.

Three days after arriving back in Liberia, barely three weeks after my fateful meeting with Bentley outside the seminary library in Denver, and a decade and a half since I'd last laid eyes on Mama stalking away in anger from the celebration of the Bible translation in Balumah, I found myself riding in the back of the Land Cruiser nearing the place where I hoped I would finally get the chance to meet face to face with her again.

Would Mama be well? What did she look like now? Would she be willing to sit with me and talk? She was no longer young, and I worried about the impact time and the wars would have had on her. I was concerned she might not even remember what I looked like. I'd had difficulty myself recognizing the few old acquaintances I'd seen since my return, so great had been the effects of extended trauma, malnutrition, and starvation on their bodies.

"You nervous, Tony?" Bentley shifted in his seat and look out at our surroundings.

"Petrified."

"It'll be okay," he said. "I have a feeling everything's going to be all right."

His confidence was calming. I couldn't have been more thankful for Bentley being with me. His generosity had made all of this possible, and while his tall, white presence made it impossible to maintain a low profile, it would also afford me a level of protection when it came to meeting with my family, since in Liberia as in most cultures the first inclination and custom was always to treat guests with politeness and respect.

The going was slow once we reached Matavi as the Land Cruiser had to negotiate narrow alleys congested by the debris of artillery shelling, stripped-down abandoned vehicles, and countless pedestrians. Garbage was piled everywhere, stalked by swarms of flies. But despite all this, I saw children running and playing in the streets.

Dozens of them, in fact, seemed to have been watching for us because they came pouring out from adjacent streets and alleyways to surround our vehicle. There were so many our driver was forced to stop. Many had bloated bellies from malnutrition and parasites, but that hadn't slowed them down. They were all singing, jumping, laughing, and dancing with hands raised above their heads.

Some of the youngest ones ran around in circles as if they didn't know what to do with their bodies. Their skin tone was coal black like my own, their matchstick-thin little bodies clad in ragged T-shirts and occasionally a pair of shorts. Waving to them out the window, I once again saw a reflection of my younger self. I wished I felt like celebrating with them.

Then I caught sight of my sister Victoria wading through the mob of children outside. I rolled the window down.

"You made it!" she hollered over the bedlam. "You're in the right place."

"Wonderful." I tried not to sound as apprehensive as I felt.

Victoria looked around at all of the children. "As you can see, word travels fast around here."

"Is everything okay?"

"Yes," she said. "I think we're ready. Mama will see you now."

With that, our driver broke into singing. It was a spontaneous Liberian rendition of "How Great Thou Art" with its melodious, singsong rhythm. His joyous music reminded of something I hadn't thought much about lately. Despite our past history and present troubles, we Liberians are at heart a celebratory people. Jesus through his Holy Spirit was indeed still sowing joy here in the midst of so much pain and suffering, even among people living within the shadows of ruin.

I smiled at the driver. "You just keep singing, my friend. Maybe it will rub off on everybody."

"Yes, sir-o!"

Bentley turned his head toward me as he waved through the window at the excited children. "I should have asked this earlier, Tony. Does your mother speak English?"

"She does, but she may not want to."

"What language will we be speaking then?"

"Probably Belle, my father's language."

"Oh, great. How's your Belle?"

"Still pretty good, I hope."

"Me, too. Because I have no idea what any of these children are saying."

"They're singing a welcome."

"Really? That sounds encouraging."

"Everyone is happy," the driver said. "It's only a couple more blocks. But I can take this vehicle no farther."

"Okay," I said. "I guess we're walking."

Shouts of joy erupted as I pushed open the car door. Bentley, Victoria, and I were all mobbed by the children, along with a number of adults who'd joined them now. Everyone was clapping and laughing, reaching out to touch us or to try to shake our hands. I felt carried along by the crowd, trying to take everything in as we moved down the street with our exuberant escorts toward a row of ramshackle buildings.

The physical conditions of this shantytown were even worse than I'd imagined with broken-down hovels and the corrugated metal and scavenged boards of makeshift shanties. The narrow street itself was packed mud. A strong smell of urine, rotting garbage, and unwashed perspiration stung at my nostrils.

Part of me wanted to break down and cry over this place where Mama had ended up. Tears for Balumah and our lost village home. Tears for the terror and the chaos and the killing. Tears for this lost culture and broken land. Tears for harsh religion, my own need for repentance, and our many years of estrangement and separation.

As we drew abreast of the house where Mama lived, Victoria broke through the crowd and ran on ahead. People packed the street all around us, cheering. Then I saw Mama.

Dressed in a plain black robe with a bright red-and-white-striped scarf tied around her head, Mama shuffled slowly out her front door to stand on the porch. Her body was stooped and frail under the enveloping black material, her face creased with age, but her brown eyes were as compelling and direct as I remembered.

At the moment, they overflowed with tears, and I could see her swallowing as she tried to speak. The cheers of the crowd were so loud that I couldn't hear the words that emerged. But it didn't matter because I could read her lips.

"My son!" she was saying. "My son!"

CHAPTER FORTY

No Ghost

The next thing I knew, I was standing on the makeshift porch of her tiny shanty, embracing Mama. As I held her in my arms, I could see more clearly how much she'd changed. She had an unsightly gap in her teeth. What hair I could see peeking out from her scarf had turned white. Her cheekbones and collar bones thrust out like photos I'd seen of famine victims, and she'd lost so much weight I felt I could lift her into the air with one hand.

Holding on to my arm, Mama reached up to feel my forehead and run her fingers across my cheek. At her touch, I felt a wave of guilt for all we'd lost and that I hadn't been there for all she'd been through.

"Kono," she said softly, invoking my childhood name. "Are you real?"

"Yes, Mama." I was crying. Everyone around us was in tears. I found out later that among them were extended family relatives living in and around Monrovia whom Victoria had gathered together for this reunion. I didn't recognize many of them, and it turned out that most of them hadn't recognized me either.

Mama kept running her hands all over me to see if I was real. Then she pulled away from me with a grin and motioned playfully, indicating she wanted to give me—a forty-plus-year-old man!—a piggyback ride as if to make sure I was the same Tony she'd carried on her back when I was young.

Everyone laughed.

As we continued talking, Mama spoke in Belle. Despite her physical deterioration and all she'd been through, her voice sounded as strong as ever. Victoria stood by translating for Bentley. "They told me you were dead, Tony. Maybe you are a ghost."

"No, Mama. No ghost."

She reached up to feel the collar of my golf shirt. "You are dressed sharp, my son."

I laughed. "It's just a shirt."

"But this other man, this big *toubabou* [white man] with you—maybe *he* is a ghost?"

"Mama, this is my friend Bentley."

"Ah. I have heard about this man from Victoria. Everyone here says your friend is an American doctor."

"That's right."

"Has he come to work in the clinic?"

"No, he's not here for the clinic. He and I studied together in America, and he came with me because we're friends. "

She nodded. I wasn't sure how much she understood, but at the moment it wasn't important. We all entered her home and sat down on the floor cushions to talk. I felt a love radiating from Mama I knew was genuine, and it was all I could do to keep from breaking down and weeping some more. We weren't here to talk about religion. We were here because of what we felt for one another.

Mama paid special attention to Bentley as if she somehow sensed he was partly responsible for bringing me here to see her. Since we were her guests, some food was brought out—a large bowl of soup. There was only one spoon. Mama began eating some of the soup with the spoon, then stopped and handed the bowl and spoon to Bentley.

While this was normal practice in our society, where people passed around a communal bowl and shared the same utensil, it was hardly a norm in America. But Bentley didn't hesitate. Accepting the bowl and spoon from Mama, he dipped the spoon into the soup and took a big sip. Mama and everyone else beamed. Now Bentley was one of us.

Victoria eventually asked if Bentley might consider examining Mama, as she'd been having some stomach trouble. Again without hesitation, Bentley agreed. After performing a rudimentary physical check and listening to Mama's heart, he made some recommendations about diet and natural treatments, since he knew well that actual pharmaceuticals were severely limited.

"So how is your stomach today?" I asked Mama.

Her wide smile lit up her face. "Nothing can take away my joy today, son."

I was so overcome with emotion that I didn't know what to say. It was a reminder of all of the changes war brings. So much gets stripped away, and what we have left are whatever connections with people we've been able to cling to, even with those from whom we've been estranged.

Food and drink were brought out as we continued to talk. By now, I'd greeted the other family members who were there.

This included my uncle Joseph Tanjoe, who with the deaths of my Uncle Sekou and others had become the family patriarch. With respect for his position, I said to him: "I've been away for so many years. What news here?"

Uncle Joseph willingly began a history of all of the events that had taken place within the family since I had last been in Liberia. Mama sat and listened with us, interjecting now and then to give her perspective or offer more detail. As the time wore on, the conversation finally lagged. We all sat and watched the children, who were still swarming and playing outside in front of the wooden porch.

Mama reached across to put her hand on mine. "So why else have you returned to us today, Tony?"

"I came for you, Mama. I came to see you."

"You came all this way just to see me?"

"Of course," I said. "I wanted to see you."

Now it was her turn to be at a loss for words, wiping tears from the corner of her eyes with the back of her gnarled hand.

By the time we were ready to leave, the late afternoon sun had begun to dip low in the west. The crowds outside had dispersed enough that our driver was able to bring the Land Cruiser up the street to park right in front of Mama's house. Mama nodded toward the vehicle. "Looks like someone has sent a car for you."

"Yes," I said. "From where we're staying at the radio station."

"ELWA?"

"That's right," I said, surprised.

"I remember all of your broadcasts."

"Really?" I hadn't realized Mama had ever listened to them. I exchanged glances with Victoria, who said nothing. Mama rose with what seemed like great difficulty from where she'd been sitting. I held out my arms to her, and we came together again, hugging one another in a long embrace.

"Will you come back to see me again, Tony?" Mama asked.

"Yes," I promised her. "I will."

CHAPTER FORTY-ONE

This Is My Son

I did return, but as it turned out, I would only see Mama one more time before she died. Over the next two years, I corresponded periodically with family members, and we were able to raise some money to send to my family.

Then in 2006, Bentley and I flew back to Liberia. Conditions had improved enough that Bentley brought his teenage daughter along as well. The purpose for this trip was for me to purchase land and begin setting up a new nonprofit ministry to serve victims of the Liberian civil wars. We were also able to bring in some much-needed medical equipment along with food and medical supplies.

Mama seemed even more elated to see me a second time and to see Bentley again, too. She asked about Beth and our children and wanted to hear all about our life in America. Her house was busy with many people coming and going.

"This is my son," she kept telling anyone who would listen. "This is my son."

By this point, Liberia had started a long, slow journey toward healing that continues to this day. The country elected the first female head of state in Africa, President Ellen Johnson Sirleaf. The UN began investing large amounts of money to help restore the nation. Beth's book about her own Liberian experience was also coming along well by then, and we were working to set up a long-term ministry and a school for girls on the outskirts of Monrovia.

Back in America, I continued my work with SIM, teaching and traveling and speaking to churches and other groups. I'd also been working toward becoming an American citizen, hoping my dual citizenship would help us in our ministry to West Africa.

Ten months later, I was working on the computer one night when my cell phone rang. It was my sister Victoria calling from Liberia. She had sad news to share. Mama had passed away.

My eyes welled up with tears. Not that the news was completely unexpected—we'd heard from others in the family that Mama hadn't been well of late—but I hadn't expected her life to end so suddenly. As strong and determined as she'd always been, it was hard to come to terms with the fact that Mama was gone.

I cannot remember everything, but I remember what matters.

I remember Mama as she was in my earliest memories, standing young and resilient in the morning African light, her eyes ablaze with love and belief in her children and in her God.

I remember Mama always rushing to protect me as best she could against what was evil, even through the pain of losing me for a time.

I remember Mama as I last saw her, still indomitable in

spirit despite her frailty, but softened by war's dark nightmares and comprehending at last that she hadn't really lost me at all and I hadn't lost her. Despite our differences, our two hearts could still connect under the influence and imprint of a God full of grace and infinite love.

"The funeral will be in two days," Victoria informed me. "Tony, can you come?"

CHAPTER FORTY-TWO

Turning Hearts

Thirty-six hours after the phone call from Victoria, my plane touched down once again at Roberts Field. I'd slept some on the flight, but not nearly enough, and I felt emotionally and physically drained. Thankfully, SIM had once again graciously arranged for me to stay at the ELWA guesthouse. A driver from ELWA met me at the airport and would shuttle me back and forth from the campus to Mama's funeral.

Funerals of all types in Liberia are often elaborate affairs stretching over a number of days with flowers everywhere, people dressed in their finery, live music with trumpets and other instruments, and multiple celebrations of the dead one's life. Since Mama was Muslim, I supposed that her funeral would involve elements of folk Islamic tradition as well.

I arrived at the ELWA guesthouse to find a message waiting for me from Victoria. When I reached her by phone, she let me know that Mama's funeral ceremony would be tomorrow at ten a.m. at St. Peter's Lutheran Church in Monrovia.

I knew St. Peter's had been reopened, but was surprised to hear this news. "You are having Mama's funeral in a Christian church?"

"Mama said that's what she wanted," Victoria said.

"Mama wanted this?" I was even more surprised. "Did she tell you why?"

"No, I never asked her. Mama's changed some over the past few years. I assumed it must have something to do with what St. Peter's has come to mean for Liberia—because of the massacre."

"Okay. I'll plan to get there early."

Thoroughly exhausted, I dropped into bed that night and fell into a deep sleep. I dreamt of many bits and fragments. Mama's face. The jungle. Our rice fields. The river we walked along between Balumah and our farm. Once again, I saw the rice kitchen burning to the ground. But it no longer seemed to matter because my grandmother and Mama were there and both of them had their arms around me. My father was there too.

Somewhere in my dreams, it dawned on me that through every lost life, through every lost connection, and through those who'd disappeared and those who remained, God was still at work, turning hearts as a farmer turns the earth before planting, sowing seeds of his unfathomable love.

CHAPTER FORTY-THREE

St. Peter's Rite

The ELWA driver dropped me off at St. Peter's Lutheran Church early the next morning. It was well before the funeral was scheduled to begin, and the doors to the building hung open to reveal rows of empty pews.

I was apparently the first to arrive. Walking into the sanctuary, I looked around at the pews and other fixtures still under restoration. So many innocent people had died here a decade and a half before. I would never fully understand why such things happened, how justice could ever be served, or how life could even go on for the survivors. Yet life did go on. Worship continued to rise out of darkness and ashes.

Mama's casket was already in place, resting on risers at the front of the church and surrounded by hundreds of flowers. I approached the closed coffin and reached out to touch the metal lid. Since the church had no air conditioning, it was warm to the touch.

Bowing my head, I cried out in prayer on behalf of Mama's soul. No matter what, the bond we shared had made a difference—at least to me. I was who I was in large part because of who she was. Removing my hand from the casket, I walked over to a pew and sat down.

"You must be Tony."

Turning my head, I saw a stocky man with a dark beard and warm smile emerging from a door beside the altar. He was about my age and wore a minster's black robe under a purple clergy stole with gold embroidery crosses.

"Yes, I'm Tony."

"Your sister Victoria has told me all about you." Approaching me, he shook my hand, then introduced himself as an associate pastor here at St. Peter's. "She told me all about your family too. How you left Islam and went to African Bible College. How you worked for ELWA and escaped the war and went to live in the United States. And how you came back to Liberia a couple of years ago to reconnect with your mother."

I nodded.

"I imagine it feels somewhat strange for you to be here now."

"Yes, it does," I said. "Do you know why my mother wanted her funeral to be held here in a church? I mean—"

"You mean because she was Muslim," he finished for me.

"Exactly."

"She was Muslim on the outside at least. I can't tell you exactly why she wanted the funeral to be here. But I can tell you this. A couple of years ago, not long after your reunion with her, your mother started showing up here during Sunday services."

"She actually joined in the services?" My first thought was what a risk she'd taken as a Mandingo woman to appear at a place of regular Christian worship. What fears she must have had to overcome.

"Not entirely," the pastor responded. "At least not that I ever saw. She would simply slip in through the vestibule every now and then in the middle of a service and sit quietly in the back, then slip out without speaking to anyone before the service ended. Sometimes she would just stand in the back. I saw her quite a few times back there. She was always by herself, and I could tell she was Muslim by her dress. I didn't know her story, but I sensed she was searching for something."

I didn't know how to respond. The last time I'd seen Mama, she hadn't mentioned anything about coming here. The pastor's gaze turned toward the back of the church where others were beginning to arrive for the ceremony. Then he turned back to me.

"Anyway, I wasn't all that surprised when I was told your mother wanted to have her funeral here at St. Peter's. Even less so after your sister told me your story. I hope this gives you some peace, Brother Weedor."

He left me alone to go greet the new arrivals. I looked back at the altar and Mama's casket and all at once found myself weeping uncontrollably like a child. I suppose in many ways I was still the same lost boy from a broken family and a broken country full of rain.

I was still crying a few minutes later when Victoria arrived with a number of other family members and Mama's friends. I cried when the church filled to near overflowing with mourners. I cried through the ceremony. My eyes even overflowed when the funeral was over and when we all went back outside.

The driver from ELWA returned to take me back to where I was staying. As we drove away, I realized I'd learned one last great lesson from Mama—that relationships spring from givings of grace. Maybe tears are the purest echoes of what we've lost. Maybe tears are how we are supposed to see the light.

And if you want to ask me if I, as a follower of Jesus, believe I will ever see my Muslim mother again in heaven, I will always remember how, on a sweltering Liberian morning in the midst of her funeral flowers, Mama made it as far as this church.

I believe she was on the way.

Tony and Manifah Gbejoe Weedor
Matavi, Liberia 2004

EPILOGUE

I often think about the ways God has protected me since coming to know Jesus more than three decades ago. At times, I've needed a shield from harm; at other times, I've needed inspiration. I've also needed propping up when I was so physically tired and emotionally spent I could barely stand. Yet through any darkness, Jesus has stood by me, closer than the closest of friends, because, as Psalm 139:12 reminds me, "Even the darkness is not dark to [him]."

When we read of Jesus's life in the Gospels, where are we likely to find him? Did he spend his days among those in power? Those with little or nothing to fear? No, we see Jesus investing his time overwhelmingly among those who are in pain, the weak, and the powerless. People who are afraid.

There have been times in the writing of this book when I've been so overcome by dark memories I've had to stop writing for a time. No one who has lost loved ones, suffered through abandonment or severe illness, been a victim of rape or physical violence, served in combat, or been forced to flee from terrorism or war can say honestly that what happened to them has left them unscarred. Jesus too had scars. He showed the wounds from his crucifixion on a Roman cross, the scars from all our hatred and inhumanity, to his disciples and many others after he was dead and buried and rose again to eternal life.

"Do not be afraid," Jesus reminds us over and over again in Scripture. "Trust in the Father and trust in me . . . Surely I am with you always, even to the end of the world."

During his first inaugural address, American President Franklin Delano Roosevelt said to the American people, "The only thing we have to fear is fear itself." He meant it as a call to courage, and his words inspired a nation. How much more inspiring then are Jesus's own words in John 14:27: "Peace I leave with you; my peace I give you. I do not give to you as the world gives. Do not let your hearts be troubled and do not be afraid."

Is fear any different now than it was in Roosevelt's time—or during the earthly lifetime of Jesus? Not really. Every generation faces its own fears and problems. We may not be facing worldwide war, but we do face worldwide terror attacks. Fear has invaded our street corners, our schools, and even our homes—just as it did for me in Liberia. Terrorism metastasizes fear.

"I am the Good Shepherd," Jesus once told his disciples (John 10:1-11). I think what he meant was *I stand in the door of the sheepfold to protect you, my people, from any and all predators. To protect you from any and all fears. As the ultimate sacrifice, I lay down my life for you, my sheep. I pay the price to defeat even death, and in so doing, I ward off all hatreds, all oppressive religiosity, all spirits of war and anger and revenge, all lies and spirits of deception, all greed and lust and unclean spirits of addiction, all jealousy and resentment and bitterness, and all emotional and physical pain. This doesn't mean you will never experience some of these things, but through me you can overcome them.*

My family and I finally settled for good in the United States. I became an American citizen in 2014, a story I hope to write more about in a future book. For many years, my wife and I have served with organizations such as SIM International and Advancing Native Missions as well as continued our ministry in Liberia and other parts of Africa. We've been able to be part of bringing much-needed medical equipment and supplies into Liberia. Through the help of many generous supporters, we have built a school for girls, Petals of Hope, on the outskirts of Monrovia. On the same property, we have also erected the first buildings for what I hope will become a spiritual retreat and study center for African pastors and Christians modeled after Francis Schaeffer's L'Abri center in Switzerland.

With the help of the United Nations, Christian ministry agencies, and many other relief organizations, Liberia has made progress on the road to recovering from its devastating civil wars. Yet some of the same issues that plagued Liberia during the civil wars remain, and in 2014, a deadly Ebola outbreak once again returned Liberia to global news headlines.

Beth and I travel back to our home country of Liberia on a regular basis. While I am not a politician and have no such aspirations, in 2016. I received the honor of being asked to speak to both houses of Congress in Liberia. My concerns are spiritual, cultural, and relational. I speak of these things regularly through my ELWA radio broadcasts that reach millions throughout West Africa. I teach about the difference between relationship and religion, the dangers of religiosity and a false faith based solely on a man-made church, and how such misplaced faith can tip into violence.

Whatever we may believe or not believe, we are all human. And it is here among our common humanity where Jesus is at work. A personal relationship with Jesus moves beyond religion, beyond all human weakness, and beyond all human power. "I am the way, the truth, and the life," Jesus tells us in John 14:6.

No matter what you may have gone through or done or how you may be suffering, Jesus' love and forgiveness are available to you. At this very moment, he remains at work in our lives and in this world through his Holy Spirit. He is still carrying out his mission of redemption. He still stands in the doorway to the sheepfold (John 10:7-9), prepared to protect any who turn to him in ways we may not yet have even begun to imagine. Fears may torment us, but his perfect love casts out our fear (1 John 4:18) if we will just reach out and take his loving outstretched hand. Call out to Jesus in faith, and you will see what I mean.

Hope rises. Fear falls.

FROM FOUNDING TO CIVIL WAR: A BRIEF HISTORY OF LIBERIA

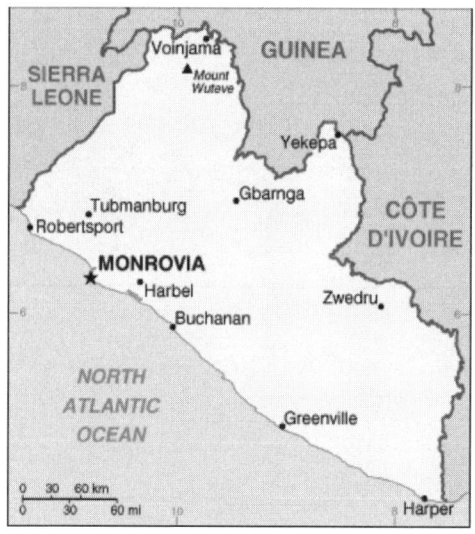

From Wikimedia Commons

Liberia is located on the west coast of Africa and bounded by the Atlantic Ocean and Gulf of Guinea as well as the modern-day countries of Sierra Leone, the Ivory Coast, and Guinea. About the size of the American state of Pennsylvania, this environmentally rich landmass includes a rainy tropical climate, beautiful beaches, rich rainforests, and valuable mineral resources. In precolonial times, Liberia was inhabited and controlled by sixteen indigenous tribes, many of which continue to play major roles in Liberia today.

Liberian history changed radically in the nineteenth century when freed slaves from America arrived. These settlers, who would become known as Americo-Liberians or Americoes, negotiated with tribal chiefs to purchase land and established a coastal settlement. Despite many hardships, the settlement thrived with continued support from America. Subsequent expansion would eventually lead to the formation in 1847 of the Republic of Liberia with a constitution and form of government modeled after that of the United States. The capital city of Monrovia was named after American President James Monroe. Despite representing less than five percent of the overall population, the Americo-Liberians in time came to dominate and control the indigenous peoples, ironically recreating through brutality, economic power, and political manipulation, the same type of American plantation culture from which they'd escaped.

Still, while representing an oppressive ruling cultural elite, the Americo-Liberians did introduce a high level development through strong relations with America and other Western powers. Liberian President William Tubman became the first African head of state to visit the White House under the administration of President Franklin Delano Roosevelt. The busy Freeport of Liberia grew up around an artificial harbor built during WWII by American military forces to ensure a continuous flow of rubber to the Allied war effort.

During the Cold War, Liberia was viewed by successive American administrations as a bulwark against Soviet expansion in Africa, and for years, the country received more American foreign aid than any other African nation. By the late 1970s, Liberia had become on the surface at least one of the most progressive countries in Africa with a physical and economic infrastructure built around the export of rubber and other natural resources.

But the concentration of Liberia's increasing wealth among the country's ruling elite, along with hoarding of resources, cronyism, and corruption, fueled growing resentment among the indigenous "country people." Tensions grew to a boiling point in 1979 during what came to be known as the rice riots in Monrovia. Hundreds of native Liberians were killed, and President Tolbert had to bring in troops from neighboring Guinea to help restore control.

One year later on April 12, 1980, a squadron of Liberian Army soldiers from the Krahn tribe led by a Krahn officer named Samuel Doe stormed Liberia's Executive Mansion and assassinated President Tolbert. Proclaiming that he was returning Liberia to its original residents, Doe began a brutal campaign of imprisonments, seizures of property, and executions against the Americo-Liberians who had for so long oppressed native tribal groups.

But Doe's regime proved at least as corrupt as its predecessors. Doe elevated many of his own Krahn tribesmen to positions of power and began to persecute other tribes who objected to such favoritism or opposed his rule. Despite continued millions in American aid, the Liberian economy began to falter, leaving the indigenous peoples suffering almost as badly as under the Americo-Liberians. Still, Doe managed to stay in power throughout the 1980s until the collapse of the Soviet Union in 1991. The end of the Cold War greatly reduced any incentive for US government support. As this source of foreign capital dried up, Doe's hold on power grew increasingly tenuous.

Into this situation stepped Charles Taylor, Doe's former minister of finance, who had fled the country under suspicion of embezzlement and mismanagement of government funds. Taylor had raised a small but well-equipped rebel army of discontented Liberians with the support and guidance of Libya's Muammar Gaddafi, and on Christmas Eve 1989, Taylor and his forces crossed over from the Ivory Coast to invade Liberia.

TRIBAL/ETHNIC GROUPS OF LIBERIA

The following are the sixteen officially recognized indigenous tribal/ethnic groups in Liberia. These groups make up 95 percent of the country's population.

- Kpelle (The largest tribe.)
- Bassa
- Gio
- Kru
- Grebo
- Mandingo (Muslims often found in trade and transport. Tony's mother's tribe.)
- Mano
- Krahn (Samuel Doe's tribe.)
- Gola (Beth's tribe. Also Charles Taylor's tribe.)
- Gbandi
- Loma
- Kissi

- Vai
- Belle (Tony's father's tribe.)
- Mende
- Dey

From Wikimedia Commons

ABOUT THE AUTHORS

 Pastor Tony Weedor has crossed many borders. As a native African and former Muslim, he brings a unique perspective to questions about cultural conflict and has brought his message to a number of churches, conferences, and seminaries throughout the world.

Tony says his story is about the enormity of God's love. He was in training to become an imam when he decided to follow Jesus. His Muslim parents disowned him as a result, and while he managed to finish college, he barely escaped a horrific civil war with his wife and their fourteen-month-old daughter. After three years in a refugee camp, they were rescued and brought to America where Tony graduated from Denver Seminary (USA). Tony holds a M Div/PR-Philosophy and has taught Islamic history both at Denver Seminary and at Evangelical Theological College in Ethiopia. He lectured about Islam following the 9/11 terrorist attacks and has spoken before Congress in his native Liberia. Today, Tony's Bible radio commentaries are heard throughout a large portion of West Africa. As a Missions Associate with Southeast Christian Church in Louisville, Kentucky, he continues teaching others how to better love and see Muslims through Jesus' eyes.

 Andy Straka is a best-selling, award-winning author.

To learn more, visit him at www.andystraka.com.

ACKNOWLEDGMENTS

My deepest thanks to my wife Beth, who has seen it all: tears of joy and tears of trial and sorrow. Her relentless love for our children and me truly makes her my Lioness of Judah. Thank you also to my children. To Abigail, our eldest child, who went through everything without realizing it and is still full of joy; to Alieya-Leechelle, the first child born on American soil; to Antoinette, our third daughter; to our son Anthony, whom we call "TJ"; to Cody Mylander, my "favorite" son-in-law; and last but not least, to my first grandson, Kaius Anthony, not because he can as yet understand the words that are written here, but because in a few years he will need them.

Thank you to my parents, Mr. Forkpah and Mrs. Manifah Gbejoe Weedor, for everything they did to help me survive. And to my Liberian siblings: the late MJ Blackie, my oldest sister; Victoria Weedor Sarnor, my youngest sister; and my brothers Austin and Alfred Weedor.

Thanks especially to Dr. Larry and Mrs. Linda Tiedje, for rescuing us from the refugee camp in La Cote D'Ivoire. To Mr. Gary and Karen Mitchel, who were the first to welcome us to Denver; they watched our kids grow. To the Reverend Ron and Pauline Sonius, God's instrument for bringing me into the Kingdom of Light, and to Reverend Les and Verla Urunh.

I would also be remiss in not thanking the individuals, organizations, and institutions that have provided me with the knowledge I've needed to engage the world: the African Bible College in Yekepa, Liberia; Evangelical Theological College in Addis Ababa, Ethiopia; the faculty members of Denver Seminary, Denver, CO, USA; Serving in Missions (SIM) and ELWA; and Advancing Native Missions, (ANM).

Finally, to all our praying and supporting churches around the world, thank you doesn't seem like a strong enough expression to tell you how grateful I am for your longtime, generous outpouring of love and support for Beth and me and our ministry.

LEARN MORE ABOUT TONY WEEDOR AND HIS MINISTRY

THEREASONFORTEARSBOOK.COM